DAVID MARSHALL LANG'S JOURNEY FROM RUSSIA TO ARMENIA VIA CAUCASIAN GEORGIA

Volume 3

THE WISDOM OF BALAHVAR

THE WISDOM OF BALAHVAR
A Christian Legend of the Buddha

Edited by
DAVID MARSHALL LANG

LONDON AND NEW YORK

First published in 1957 by George Allen & Unwin Ltd.

This edition first published in 2022
by Routledge
2 Park Square, Milton Park, Abingdon, Oxon OX14 4RN

and by Routledge
605 Third Avenue, New York, NY 10158

Routledge is an imprint of the Taylor & Francis Group, an informa business

© 1957 George Allen & Unwin and David Marshall Lang.

All rights reserved. No part of this book may be reprinted or reproduced or utilised in any form or by any electronic, mechanical, or other means, now known or hereafter invented, including photocopying and recording, or in any information storage or retrieval system, without permission in writing from the publishers.

Trademark notice: Product or corporate names may be trademarks or registered trademarks, and are used only for identification and explanation without intent to infringe.

British Library Cataloguing in Publication Data
A catalogue record for this book is available from the British Library

ISBN: 978-1-03-215852-5 (Set)
ISBN: 978-1-00-325111-8 (Set) (ebk)
ISBN: 978-1-03-216873-9 (Volume 3) (hbk)
ISBN: 978-1-03-216881-4 (Volume 3) (pbk)
ISBN: 978-1-00-325076-0 (Volume 3) (ebk)

DOI: 10.4324/9781003250760

Publisher's Note
The publisher has gone to great lengths to ensure the quality of this reprint but points out that some imperfections in the original copies may be apparent.

Disclaimer
The publisher has made every effort to trace copyright holders and would welcome correspondence from those they have been unable to trace.

THE YOUNG BUDDHA

THE WISDOM OF BALAHVAR

A Christian Legend of the Buddha

by

DAVID MARSHALL LANG
M.A., Ph.D.

Lecturer in Georgian
School of Oriental and African Studies
University of London

LONDON: GEORGE ALLEN AND UNWIN LTD

First published in 1957

This book is copyright under the Berne Convention. Apart from any fair dealing for the purposes of private study, research, criticism or review, as permitted under the Copyright Act, 1956, no portion may be reproduced by any process without written permission. Enquiry should be made to the publisher.

© George Allen & Unwin Ltd. 1957

*Printed in Great Britain
in 11pt. Baskerville type
by C. Tinling & Co. Ltd.
Liverpool, London and Prescot*

PREFACE

> All that glisters is not gold;
> Often have you heard that told:
> Many a man his life hath sold
> But my outside to behold:
> Gilded tombs do worms infold.
>
> MERCHANT OF VENICE II, viii

One might not expect to find in a play by Shakespeare an echo of the Buddha's Great Renunciation. However, the episode of the Three Caskets in *The Merchant of Venice* is but one of the many literary offshoots of the Barlaam and Ioasaph romance, a Christianized version of episodes from the Buddha's life and mission. Under the deceptive guise of an edifying account of India's conversion to Christianity, this became one of the most popular works circulating in mediaeval Christendom; a pedigree drawn up in 1896 by Joseph Jacobs shows that from an Indian, probably Buddhist Sanskrit original, the tale ultimately branched out into over eighty versions in the principal languages of Europe, the Christian Orient, and even Africa.

Of the oriental Christian versions, one of the oldest and most curious is the Georgian text entitled *The Wisdom of Balahvar*, which is here translated into English for the first time. (The only translation previously published is a Russian one.) For centuries, indeed, *The Wisdom of Balahvar* has figured prominently in Caucasian popular literature, to the extent that Balaver is even used as a Christian name in some parts of Western Georgia. Originally, the work was an abridgement made for devotional purposes from a longer Georgian text entitled *Life and Acts of the Blessed Iodasaph*, a unique eleventh century manuscript of which has recently come to light in the Greek Patriarchal Library in Jerusalem. For reasons which will be set out in the first half of the present book, there are strong reasons for believing that the story of the Blessed Iodasaph, i.e. the Bodhisattva, was adapted from an Arabic source between A.D. 800 and 900, and later served St. Euthymius the Athonite as a model for the Greek Barlaam and Ioasaph romance which became widely diffused from the eleventh century. Thus, the material now presented may contribute something towards the solution of a literary problem which has aroused considerable interest, not to say controversy, in recent years.

It would have been tempting to give, instead of the shorter *Wisdom of Balahvar*, a rendering of the original Georgian *Life of the Blessed Iodasaph*. The difficulty is that the latter text is over twice the length of *The Wisdom of Balahvar*, the difference being made up of verbose homilies on religious topics which add little to the work's literary merits. The shorter version, while modifying certain episodes, retains all the story's essential features. For the sake of completeness, three of Balahvar's parables from *The Life of the Blessed Iodasaph*, omitted in our shorter Georgian text, are reproduced separately.

The oldest complete copy of *The Wisdom of Balahvar* is contained in Manuscript No. 36 of the Georgian collection in the Greek Patriarchal Library in Jerusalem, this being a collection of lives of saints copied in the thirteenth or the fourteenth century. The best printed edition is that published by Ilia Abuladze at Tiflis in 1937 and based for the most part on more recent manuscripts in Georgian collections, though portions of the text were available in twelfth to thirteenth century fragments. The English translation has been made on the basis of a collation of Abuladze's edition with the Jerusalem manuscript, with occasional reference to the fuller Georgian text, *The Life of the Blessed Iodasaph*, also preserved in Jerusalem (Georgian Ms. No. 140). The urge to reconstruct and improve the shorter version by reference to the fuller one has, however, been resisted, and corrections have been confined to eliminating scribal errors and minor inconsistencies.

The writer thanks his colleagues at the School of Oriental and African Studies, University of London, and at the British Museum, who have expressed interest in this work and guided him where he risked getting out of his depth. Grateful thanks are expressed to the Photoduplication Service of the Library of Congress, Washington, for promptly supplying microfilms of the two Jerusalem manuscripts.

The frontispiece, showing a seventeenth century Tê-hua porcelain figure of the Buddha in the pose of meditation, is reproduced by kind permission of the Percival David Foundation of Chinese Art, University of London.

D. M. Lang

School of Oriental and African Studies
University of London
24 August, 1957

CONTENTS

PREFACE   page 5

PART ONE: FROM BODHISATTVA TO SAINT JOSAPHAT: THE METAMORPHOSIS OF A LEGEND

I	The Indian Background	11
II	The Manichaean Evidence	24
III	The Arabic Versions	30
IV	The Georgian Versions	40
V	St. Euthymius the Georgian and the Greek Barlaam Romance	56
	PEDIGREE OF BARLAAM AND JOSAPHAT	65

PART TWO: THE WISDOM OF BALAHVAR TRANSLATED FROM THE OLD GEORGIAN VERSION

THE FABLES

I	*The Trumpet of Death, The Four Caskets*	79
II	*The Sower*	81
III	*The Man and the Elephant*	81
IV	*The Man and his Three Friends*	82
V	*The King for One Year*	83
VI	*The King and the Happy Poor Couple*	84
VII	*The Rich Youth and the Poor Maiden*	87
VIII	*The Fowler and the Nightingale*	89
IX	*The Tame Gazelle*	96
X	*The Amorous Wife*	110
XI	*The Youth Who had never seen a Woman*	111

FURTHER FABLES OF BALAHVAR,
TRANSLATED FROM THE JERUSALEM GEORGIAN
TEXT

Dogs and Carrion	page 123
Physician and Patient	124
The Sun of Wisdom	124
SELECT BIBLIOGRAPHY	125
POSTSCRIPT: Mr. Graves, Mr. Podro and the Kashmir Shrine	129
INDEX	131

PART ONE
FROM BODHISATTVA TO SAINT JOSAPHAT
THE METAMORPHOSIS OF A LEGEND

CHAPTER I

THE INDIAN BACKGROUND

Among the worthies venerated in mediaeval Christendom, an honoured place was occupied by Saints Barlaam and Josaphat. To them was ascribed the second conversion of India to Christianity, undertaken when the land had relapsed once more into idolatry after the supposed mission of the Apostle Thomas. Though never officially canonized, both Barlaam and Josaphat were numbered by popular acclamation in the roll of saints recognized by the Roman Catholic Church, their day being November 27; included by the thirteenth century Dominican monk Jacobus de Voragine in the *Legenda Aurea*, their lives were subsequently incorporated in the Roman martyrology compiled by Baronius in the sixteenth century and officially sanctioned by successive Popes. In the Greek Church, Ioasaph (Josaphat), son of King Abenner of India, was commemorated on August 26. According to the menaia of St. George the Hagiorite, compiled in the eleventh century for the Iviron Monastery on Mount Athos, and also utilised in the Georgian Monastery of the Holy Cross near Jerusalem, the Blessed Iodasaph was commemorated by the Georgian Orthodox Church on May 19. The Russians, on the other hand, were accustomed to remember Barlaam and Ioasaph, as well as the latter's father, King Abenner, on November 19, though this day properly belongs to another, earlier St. Barlaam of Antioch, who was martyred under the Emperor Diocletian.

All the Western versions of the Barlaam and Josaphat romance derive from the Greek version, the edifying story of Barlaam and Ioasaph. In many of the manuscripts, the title states their biography to have been brought back from 'the inner land of the Ethiopians, called the land of the Indians' by a monk called John of the Monastery of St. Saba near Jerusalem. From the thirteenth century, this harmless fiction was elaborated into a tradition that the story was an original work by the great St. John Damascene (*c.* 676-749), composed on the basis of oral information given him by Indian holy men.

The supposed authorship of St. John Damascene, the work's exotic setting, the apt fables and the lively narrative element strongly commended the tale to mediaeval readers. More than once translated into Latin from the eleventh century onwards, the lives of Barlaam and Josaphat found their way into French, German, Italian, Spanish, Provençal, Romaic, Dutch and the Scandinavian languages. The story was often versified, or circulated in popular chap-books, while Lope de Vega made it into a play. In England, it featured in Caxton's translation of the *Golden Legend*, which he printed at Westminster in 1483. From here, no doubt, Shakespeare had the idea of using Barlaam's parable of the Four Caskets for an episode in *The Merchant of Venice*. In the East, the Greek Barlaam and Ioasaph romance was early rendered into the principal Slavonic tongues, as well as into Armenian and Christian Arabic; from the latter, it passed into Ethiopic.

After the European settlement of India, and the arrival there of Roman Catholic missionaries, certain enquiring spirits were struck by the similarity between features of the life of St. Josaphat and corresponding episodes in the life of the Buddha. As Sir Henry Yule pointed out in his edition of Marco Polo, the Portuguese writer Diogo do Couto, in describing about 1612 the exploits of his countrymen in India, remarked that Josaphat 'is represented in his legend as the son of a great king in India, who had just the same upbringing, with all the same particulars that we have recounted in the life of the Buddha . . . and as it informs us that he was the son of a great king in India, it may well be, as we have said, that *he* was the Buddha of whom they relate such marvels.'

This prescient, if topsy-turvy hint remained buried in oblivion in do Couto's book for two and a half centuries. It was not until 1859 that Laboulaye quite independently drew attention in the *Journal des Débats* to the Buddhist origins of the Barlaam and Ioasaph romance, a discovery amplified in a paper published in the following year by Felix Liebrecht.

These pioneer scholars concentrated for the most part on establishing parallels between the Barlaam romance and the *Lalita-vistara*, the version of the Buddha's life and mission then best known in Europe. It should, however, be clearly understood that the Barlaam romance is not a close translation of any Indian life of the Buddha-elect known to us; nor, in all probability, did any exact Buddhist prototype ever exist for the work in the form in which it ultimately penetrated into Western Christendom. We are, rather, dealing with a work in which the ideals of renunciation and the ascetic way of life are woven round certain salient features of the traditional life of the Buddha-elect, a whole series of extraneous fables and parables being inserted from other Indian and oriental sources in the course of the work's transmission.

The search for Indian sources for the Barlaam and Ioasaph legend is complicated by lack of precise information about the genesis of the Buddhist Sanskrit lives and legends of the Buddha, and their relatively late date. Thus, the *Lalita-vistara* was probably not completed in its present guise before the third or fourth century after Christ; according to Winternitz, it was translated into Tibetan not earlier than the ninth century. It is characterized by an almost chaotic disorder of episode, and an exaggerated profusion of the miraculous element. More helpful from this viewpoint is Aśvaghoṣa's Sanskrit verse rendering of the life of Buddha, the *Buddha-carita*. Aśvaghoṣa is reputed to have been a contemporary of King Kaniṣka (2nd century A.D.); a Chinese translation of the *Buddha-carita* was made in A.D. 414-421, a Tibetan rendering in the seventh or eighth century. His poem is notable for restraint in the presentation of miracles, harmonious moderation of language and style and a well-planned and artistic arrangement of material which is considered by competent judges to contrast favourably with the diffuse profusion of the *Lalita-vistara* and the *Mahāvastu*. Parallels may also be sought for the Barlaam romance in the commentary prefaced to the Buddhist birth stories or *Jātaka Tales*, the best-known collections of which are preserved in Pali among the Theravāda Buddhist community in Ceylon.

The salient features of the life of the Buddha-elect, as contained in the original Indian tradition, and later embodied in the Barlaam and Ioasaph romance, include the following: The Bodhisattva or Buddha-elect is born in miraculous wise to Queen Māyā, consort of King Śuddhodana, who ruled over the Śākyas of Kapilavastu. The king consults his advisers to know whether the boy will become an imperial sovereign or a wandering hermit. The great sage Asita is supernaturally informed that a wonderful prince has been born, and journeys to the royal palace to predict the child's future greatness as a holy man and a Buddha. (According to the *Jātakas*, this prediction is made by a Brahmin called Koṇḍañña, who foretells that the prince will forsake the world after the Four Omens, that is to say, a man worn out by age, a sick man, a dead body and a monk.) The king is anxious to prevent this; when the young prince is taken to the temple, the streets are cleaned and decorated beforehand, trumpets are blown and bells rung, and all cripples and blind or deformed persons cleared out of the road.

Later, King Śuddhodana has a dream in which he sees his son leaving the palace and putting on the ochre-coloured garb of an ascetic. He therefore takes stringent precautions against his son's escape, providing him with three palaces in which all forms of delight and entertainment are provided. On one occasion, however, the young prince sets out with his faithful charioteer Chandaka (or Channa) to visit a garden by the eastern gate; as they drive out, he catches sight of a broken-down, toothless and grey-haired old man leaning on a stick. Learning from Chandaka that all men who attain old age must come to this state, he returns downcast to the palace. On later trips, he sees a sick man, a corpse and a mendicant; the charioteer explains their condition to the prince, who is deeply affected.

At the suggestion of the family priest, King Śuddhodana tries to distract the prince by providing feminine allurements, but the Buddha-elect is unresponsive. Eventually, he begs his father for permission to depart, though he offers to remain if Śuddhodana can promise immunity from decay, disease and death. Since these things exceed the king's powers, he gives his son leave to go. The prince determines now to carry into effect the Great Renunciation, and orders Chandaka to saddle his horse Kaṇṭhaka. After many austerities undergone and temptations surmounted, the Bodhisattva prince takes his seat beneath the Tree of Intelligence, the Bodhi or Bo-Tree (Ficus religiosa), and is arrayed in the perfect intelligence of a Buddha.

Whereas the Indian Buddhist tradition thus provides a satisfactory narrative framework for the life and act of renunciation of the Christian Saint Josaphat (Ioasaph), the same cannot be said for the figure of his mentor Barlaam (Balahvar, Balauhar), whose preachings are a central part of the story.—'No teacher have I,' declares the Buddha: 'There is none for Me to honour.' (*Buddhacarita*, trans. Johnston, xv. 4.) In embryo, however, the intervention of Barlaam is implicit in the Fourth Omen, the Bodhisattva's encounter with the wandering holy man. To quote the *Mahāvastu* in the rendering of the late J. J. Jones, the devas 'conjured up to stand before the prince a wanderer who wore the yellow robe, whose faculties were under control, who had mastered the four postures, who did not look before him farther than a plough's length in the crowded royal street of Kapilavastu. The prince saw this wanderer and his mind grew calm at the sight. "Behold," he said, "the wisdom of one who has become a wanderer."

'When he had seen him, the prince asked the wanderer, "Noble sir, with what object did you become a wanderer?" The wanderer replied, "O prince, I became a wanderer for the sake of winning self-control, calm, and utter release."

'When the prince heard the words of the wanderer he was filled with joy, and said:—

"*Verily, now, a wanderer who, conspicuous by his flowing yellow robe, crosses the crowded royal street, his body covered by mire, dust and dirt, is like the red goose in a thicket of reeds.*" [1]

It was, of course, shortly after this encounter that the Bodhisattva, like St. Josaphat in a different context, 'grew calm with the thought of Nirvana . . . and aspired after it.'

In general, there is certainly no dearth of instances where Buddhist holy men address kings and princes on the ideals and principles of religion. An example of this to which Professor J. Brough kindly drew the writer's attention is the *Milinda-pañha*, translated from the Pali into English by T. W. Rhys Davids under the title *The Questions of King Milinda*. In this work, King Milinda, who is really the Bactrian ruler Menander, is represented as 'harassing the brethren by putting puzzles to them of heretical tendency'. He is accordingly confronted by the venerable Nāgasena, 'learned, able and wise, of subdued manners, yet full of courage, versed in the traditions, a master of language, and ready in reply, one who understands alike the spirit and the letter of the law, and can expound its difficulties and refute objections to perfection'.[2] Some of Nāgasena's utterances foreshadow the ascetic Barlaam's views on the worthlessness of the human body:

> Without cleaving to it do they (the recluses) bear about the body for the sake of righteousness of life. The body, O king, has been declared by the Blessed One to be like a wound. And therefore merely as a sore, and without cleaving to it, do the

---

[1] *The Mahāvastu*, II, London, 1952, p. 152. (*Sacred Books of the Buddhists*, Vol. XVIII.)

[2] *The Questions of King Milinda*, I, Oxford, 1890, pp. 23, 36. (*Sacred Books of the East*, Vol. XXXV.)

recluses bear about the body. For it has been said by the Blessed One: "Covered with clammy skin, an impure thing and foul, Nine-apertured, it oozes, like a sore."[1]

At the conclusion of the sage Nāgasena's discourses (II. 373-4), 'Milinda the king was filled with joy of heart, and all pride was suppressed within him'. It is possible to detect a similarity to Barlaam's metaphors of the precious gems of truth when we read further that Milinda 'became aware of the virtue that lay in the religion of the Buddhas, he ceased to have any doubt at all in the Three Gems (i.e., the Buddha, his religion, and his order), he tarried no longer in the jungle of heresy, he renounced all obstinacy', and so on. Finally Milinda emulates the Great Renunciation of Gautama Buddha himself, as later reflected in the Barlaam and Ioasaph legend: 'And afterwards, taking delight in the wisdom of the Elder, he handed over his kingdom to his son, and abandoning the household life for the houseless state, grew great in insight, and himself attained to Arahatship!'

At the same time, too much should not be made of *The Questions of King Milinda* as a parallel or possible source for the Barlaam and Ioasaph romance, since virtually none of Nāgasena's parables recur in the Christian Barlaam or even in its Arabic prototype. Those of Barlaam's parables which are of Indian origin have been traced to quite different works, such as the *Mahābhārata* and the *Pancatantra*, and are mixed up with others of various provenance.

So far, attention has been directed mainly to the Barlaam legend's narrative framework, and its Buddhistic prototypes. What of the ethical principles and religious doctrine expounded by Barlaam (Balahvar) and other Christian protagonists in the story? Can any specifically Buddhist teachings be recognized under the Christian disguise assumed by the story of the Bodhisattva in the course of its migration towards the West?

Buddhism is sometimes thought of as fundamentally atheistic in character. Yet while laying emphasis on the impermanence of all physical things, the Buddha saw over against this ever-changing world something that could never change. What the hermit Barlaam called the Heavenly Paradise of God, the Buddha called 'deathlessness, peace, the unchanging state of Nirvana'—'an unborn, not become, not made, uncompounded.'[2] Thus the Buddha

---
[1] Ibid., p. 115.
[2] R. C. Zaehner, *Mysticism Sacred and Profane*, Oxford, 1957, p. 126.

recognized that there exists an eternal being transcending time, space and change; and in the urge to forsake the temporal for the eternal, Buddhist and Christian asceticism, in spite of their differing theological bases, are often at one.

So it is that despite the composite, indeed disparate elements of which the Christian legend of Barlaam and Ioasaph is composed, it manages to retain a surprisingly large element of the authentic teachings of Gautama Buddha. Anyone who cares to turn to Woodward and Mattingly's translation of the Greek Barlaam and Ioasaph romance, or to the Georgian text translated in this present volume, cannot fail to light upon passages where the Christian homilies of Barlaam (Balahvar) reproduce almost verbatim arguments which the Buddha used when preaching the need for 'suppression' and self-abnegation for the attainment of Nirvana. For purposes of comparison, some characteristic verses from E. H. Johnston's rendering of the *Buddha-carita* have been grouped below; it will be seen that they anticipate to a remarkable degree Barlaam's basic arguments and often, his very phraseology.[1]

The impermanence of the world

xxvii. 32. By teaching everything to be impermanent and without self and by denying the presence of the slightest happiness in the spheres of existence, He raised aloft the banner of His fame and overturned the lofty pillars of pride.

xx. 34. Therefore, inasmuch as the world is impermanent and given to sensual pleasures, which are transitory as a flash of lightning, and as it stands on the fingertips of Death, man should not undergo the fruit of not following the Law.

35. Those various kings, who were like Great Indra, fought even in the divine battles and were mighty and proud, yet in course of time suffering was their lot.

36. Even the earth that supports all beings is destroyed, and Meru is burnt up by the cosmic fire; the mighty ocean dries up, how much more then does the world of man, transitory as foam, go to destruction?

---

[1] Dr. A. L. Basham kindly drew the writer's attention to the importance of Aśvaghoṣa's work in this connection.

37. The wind blows violently and yet dies down, the sun scorches the world and yet goes to its setting, the fire too blazes and yet becomes extinguished; all that is, I ween, is in such case and subject to change.

38. This body, though long guarded with care and cherished with various enjoyments, yet abiding here but a few days. . . .

The impurity of the human body

xxiv. 25. There is no attachment to the body for him who sees the impurity in the body, enveloped as it is with bones, skin, blood, sinews, flesh, hair, etc.

Mankind's impotence

xviii. 47. If Man were the cause with respect to the effect, everyone would certainly obtain whatever he wanted; yet in this world some desires remain unfulfilled, and against their will men get what they do not want.

49. If Man were the agent in the world, he would certainly do what is agreeable to himself, not what is disagreeable; yet in the execution of his wishes the undesired is done as well as the desired, and who, if he were the controller of events, would carry out the undesired?

51. Man has no dominion over himself but is subject to others; for we see the effects of cold, heat, rain, thunderbolts and lightning to frustrate his efforts. Therefore Man is not master over the effects.

Worthlessness of earthly existence

xviii. 12. Know this world to be suffering and transitory, and observing mankind to be entirely burnt up with the fire of Time as with a real fire, hold existence and annihilation alike to be undesirable.

13. Know this world to be empty, without 'I' or 'mine', like an illusion, and considering this body as merely the product of the factors, think of it as consisting only of the elements.

14. Shake your mind free from transitory existence. . . .

The agony of human life

xv. 39. Birth, old age, disease and eke death, separation from what is desired, union with what is not desired, failure to attain the longed for end, these are the varied sufferings that men undergo.

40. In whatever state a man be existing, whether he is subject to the lusts or has conquered self, whether he has or has not a body, whatever quality is lacking to him, know that in short to be suffering.

Vanity of worldly glory

xx. 15. Lord of men, when Time binds and drags away the king, neither relations nor friends nor sovereignty will follow you; all will depart, afflicted and helpless. Your deeds alone will accompany you like a shadow.

16. Therefore guard your kingdom according to the Law, if you desire Paradise and a good reputation. For there is no kingdom at all in Paradise for the king who in his delusion misapplies the Law.

Vicissitudes of fortune

xix. 23. Knowing the world to be restless as the waves of the sea and meditating on it, you should take no joy in the spheres of existence, and should practise that act which is virtuous and leads to the highest good, in order to destroy the power of the act.

25. Know the bliss of salvation to be the supreme bliss. . . .

26. Look therefore on the world as encompassed with great dangers like a house on fire, and seek for that state which is tranquil and certain, and in which there is neither birth nor death, neither toil nor suffering.

Worthlessness of pleasure and ambition

xxiv. 26. The idea of pleasure is overcome by him who sees that the sensations are but suffering, each arising from their respective causes.

xxvi. 54. The suffering which comes to him whose desires are great does not come to him whose desires are small. Therefore smallness of desire should be practised, and especially so by those who seek for the perfection of the virtues.

55. He who does not fear the rich at all is not afraid of the sight of stingy people; for he obtains salvation, whose desires are small and who is not cast down on hearing that there is nothing for him.

56. If you desire salvation, practise contentment; with contentment there is bliss here and it is the Law. The contented sleep peacefully even on the ground, the discontented are burnt up even in Paradise.

57. The discontented man, however rich, is always poor, and the contented man, however poor, is always rich. The discontented man, seeking the beloved objects of sense, creates suffering for himself by toiling to obtain satiety.

The evil of passion

xxiii. 39. By reason of passion man seeks pleasure and for the sake of pleasure does evil; through doing evil he falls into Hell. There is no enemy equal to passion.

40. From passion arises desire, and from desire attachment to the lusts. From the lusts man comes to suffering. There is no adversary equal to passion.

The conquest of sin

xxiii. 28. He whose mind is overcome by the sins loses everything in life. Taking your stand on discipline, destroy the sins and cherish faith.

31. Arrogance destroys self-respect, grief steadfastness, and old age beauty, and the thought of self destroys the roots of the virtues.

33. That man is not held to be wise, who in ephemeral states of being deems himself to be the best and thinks that he is not vile.

The elimination of the ego

xx. 45. Since the world comes to birth by reason of passion and thereby undergoes much great suffering, therefore when a man can detach himself from the sphere of passion, he is no longer attached to suffering and ceases to be afflicted.

xv. 45. Know suppression to be that in which there is not either birth, or old age, or death, or fire, or earth, or water, or space, or wind, which is without beginning or end, noble and not to be taken away, blissful and immutable.

In addition to the general echoes of Buddhistic ideas which make themselves heard in Barlaam's discourses, some of his apologues have their root in Buddhistic imagery. Thus, the parable of the swimmer and his friend (extant in the Arabic version) may be compared with *Buddha-carita*, xv. 9: 'When a man is being carried away by a stream, he who, standing on dry land, does not try to pull him out, is no hero.' Balahvar's metaphor of the sun of wisdom, which is included in the present volume, has its prototype in the Buddha's 'sun of right views' (*ibid.*, xv. 35). Finally, Balahvar's parable of the good physician and his patient, also included in the present book, has an antecedent in *Buddha-carita*, xv. 10, and an even better one in xv. 32:—

Just as the individual who is overcome by illness is not cured by eating unwholesome food, so how shall he, who is overcome by the disease of ignorance and is addicted to the lusts, reach religious peace?

A like comparison may be made with *Buddha-carita*, xxiii. 54-6:—

Thus the Buddha, seeing them at that time to be full of sin, had compassion on them and reproved them with His sermon.

Just as, when people are ill, the doctor prescribes medicine for them according to their constitutions, in order to cure the disease.

So the Sage, knowing the dispositions of beings who are afflicted by the disease of passion, old age, etc., gave them the medicine of knowledge of the real truth.

Just as Ioasaph converts his father, King Abenner, in the Barlaam and Ioasaph romance, so in the *Buddha-carita* does Gautama Buddha compass the salvation of his father, King Śuddhodana. Both parents welcome their conversion in similar terms, Śuddhodana exclaiming:—

xix. 30. 'Wise and fruitful are Your deeds, in that You have released me from great suffering. I, who formerly rejoiced in the calamitous gift of the earth for the increase of grief, now rejoice in the fruit of having a son,

31. 'Rightly You went away, abandoning sovereign glory. Rightly You toiled with great labour, and rightly, beloved as You were, You left Your dear relations and have had compassion on us.

32. 'For the good of the distressed world You have also obtained this final beatitude, which not even the divine seers or the royal seers arrived at in olden times.

33. 'If You had become a universal monarch, You would not have caused me such joy as I now firmly feel by the sight of these magic powers and of Your Law.'

The farewell homily which Ioasaph (Iodasaph) addresses to his successor Barachias (Barakhia) in the Barlaam romance is perfectly in harmony with the Buddha's own teachings on the duties of princes. Thus, in his discourse addressed to King Prasenajit in the *Buddha-carita*, Gautama bids him:—

xx. 19. Thus do not harass human beings, never give free play to your senses; do not consort with the vicious or give way to anger, do not let your mind wander on evil courses.

20. Do not trouble virtuous people through pride, do not oppress ascetics who are to be treated as friends, do not undertake holy vows under the influence of sin, and do not adhere at all to evil views.

21. Do not resort to the marvellous, be not addicted to evil deeds, be not affected by arrogance, do not listen with displeasure or intolerance, do not exhaust your fame or fix your mind on falsehood, do not take land revenue in excess of the share allowed by the laws.

22. Keep your mind level and carry out the Law, consort with the good and so act that, having obtained this eminence (as king now), you may arrive again (in the next life) at a noble position.

In general, therefore, it may be said that Buddhist tradition provides most of the narrative framework for the Barlaam and Ioasaph romance, while the scriptures in which are enshrined the teachings of Gautama Buddha provide remarkably close parallels for the arguments used by the Christian hermit in converting the king's son. At the same time, a great deal in the Barlaam story remains to be accounted for, especially since the Buddha, unlike Ioasaph, had no teacher to initiate him into the mysteries of religious faith, and furthermore, since Barlaam's apologues do not occur in connected form in any Buddhist work and some of them are obviously of extraneous provenance.

It is to be concluded, accordingly, that the Barlaam and Ioasaph romance, as it eventually took shape in Greek and was thereafter diffused throughout Western Christendom, is a composite, synthetic work, built up stage by stage on the basis of genuine Buddhist tradition, but modified and expanded under the impact of external sources during the story's migration from India to the West. It certainly did not assume its final form within India, so that it is unrealistic to follow the mediaeval scholastics who imagined the Barlaam romance to have been brought direct from India to Jerusalem by St. John of Damascus, who never went there in any case. Nor can one take seriously the alternative proposition that Indian holy men came all the way to Jerusalem to relate the story orally to the great Damascene in their own idiom, for him to write down and embellish in Greek. Theories as touchingly simple as these leave out of account a whole train of evidence which now falls to be presented and considered.

CHAPTER II

THE MANICHAEAN EVIDENCE

Among the regions into which Buddhism penetrated during the centuries following its founder's death was Central Asia, including what is nowadays called Chinese Turkestan. Thence, its influence spread among the peoples living in adjacent areas, including the Iranian-speaking Soghdians whose homeland was the district round Samarkand and Bukhara. According to Clement of Alexandria, Buddhist holy men were numerous in Bactria during the second century after Christ; thence their influence penetrated into Persia. They were said to have deified the founder of their religion, and were alleged to pay homage to relics of their god buried beneath a pyramid.

In a general sense, the Classical world had become acquainted with the Buddhist religion at the time of Alexander the Great's expedition to India. Clement of Alexandria informs us that scholars who subsequently travelled thither were impressed by what they saw of hermits living in the woods, feeding on herbs and fruit, and abstaining from wine and sexual intercourse. (Adapting Prakrit or Middle Indian *samana*, 'an ascetic', which generally excludes Brahmins, the Classical sources refer to Buddhist holy men, whom they also distinguish from Brahmins, as 'Samanians', a designation later taken over by the Arabic geographers.) Elements of Buddhist teachings were evidently absorbed by the Gnostic philosophers who foreshadowed and influenced the ideas of Mani himself. Thus, the Elkesaites, whose books were favoured by the Sabaeans of Mesopotamia among whom Mani was educated, believed in successive incarnations of Our Saviour. Indian ambassadors visiting Heliogabalus provided Bardaisan with data on Buddhist asceticism, leading him to praise the abstinence of the 'Samanian' or Buddhist hermits who lived on nothing but fruit, rice and flour.[1]

Mani, a native of Mesopotamia, was born in A.D. 216 and martyred under the Sasanian king Bahram I in 274. To preach the new faith which he proclaimed he is said to have undertaken

[1] See Prosper Alfaric, *Les écritures manichéennes*, Paris, 1918-19, II, 211-27.

extensive missionary journeys into Transoxiana, Western China and India—areas in which the Buddhist creed already had strong roots. In a well-known passage cited by al-Bīrūnī from the beginning of Mani's book, the *Shābūhragān*, the founder of Manichaeism declares:

'Wisdom and deeds have always from time to time been brought to mankind by the messengers of God. So in one age they have been brought by the messenger called Buddha to India, in another by Zarādusht to Persia, in another by Jesus to the West. Thereupon this revelation has come down, this prophecy in this last age, through me, Mani, messenger of the God of truth to Babylonia.'

It is significant that, as my colleague Dr. Mary Boyce kindly informs me, among the titles given to Mani in Middle Iranian Manichaean hymns is that of Bodhisattva ('Bwdysdf'). So convinced, indeed, were some Fathers of the early Church of the heresiarch Mani's connection with the Buddha that they included both of them in a common anathema.

It would be rash to assume that Mani himself studied at first hand the sacred books of Buddhism. It was rather when Manichaeism later spread through Central Asia and became the dominant religion in areas formerly permeated by Buddhism that the Manichaeans were led to make a thorough study of the life and teachings of Gautama Buddha. Manichaeism was, after all, a syncretic and an adaptable faith. In the West, it assumed a Christian colouring; in the Near East, it borrowed elements from the ancient Babylonian and Zoroastrian religions. Likewise, in Central Asia, the Manichees absorbed elements of the Buddhist religion, many of which were by no means incompatible with their own ideals.

Professor R. C. Zaehner has recently reminded us that 'Manichaeism equates evil with matter, good with spirit, and is therefore particularly suitable as a doctrinal basis for every form of asceticism and many forms of mysticism'. From the Manichaean standpoint, 'the body is composed of the substance of evil . . . it is a prison and a carcase'.[1] Now this is precisely the idea which infuses the story of Barlaam and Ioasaph; we shall find it prominent in the Georgian text translated in this present volume; it is fully de-

---

[1] Zaehner, *The Teachings of the Magi*, London, 1956, pp. 53-4. For the elucidation of the Manichaean evidence, I have enjoyed the advantage of personal advice from Professor W. B. Henning, to whom thanks are expressed.

veloped even in the Arabic non-Christian version, *The Book of Balauhar and Budhasaf*. The devotees of a creed like Manichaeism, who professed to regard the human body as a carrion, would naturally be attracted especially to those features of Buddhist teaching in which, to quote Nāgasena's words to King Milinda, man's body is represented as 'an impure thing and foul'.

If one examines the course of conduct laid down for the 'Elect' Manichee, as distinct from the lay adherent or 'Hearer', one finds precepts recalling the life of the Buddhist monk on the one hand, and the Christian ascetic on the other, but most peculiarly similar to the austerities practised by Balahvar/Barlaam. Thus, while all Manichees were vegetarians, the Elect abstained from wine, from marriage and from property. They were supposed to possess no more than food for one day and clothes for one year. Their obligation not to produce fresh life or to take it was so absolute that it extended to the vegetable kingdom: they might neither sow nor reap, nor even break their bread themselves, 'lest they pain the Light which was mixed with it.' So they went about, as Indian holy men do, with a disciple who prepared their food for them.[1] It would be hard to think of anyone who fulfilled these prescriptions more faithfully than the hermit Balahvar, with his single tattered hair garment, wandering in the desert and existing on a diet of herbs.

Since the German Turfan expeditions of half a century ago, it has become abundantly clear that traces of the early development of the Barlaam and Ioasaph legend must be sought for in those areas of Central Asia where Buddhism and Manichaeism for a time overlapped. Two fragments of Aśvaghoṣa's *Buddha-carita* were recovered by the Turfan expeditions from Šorčuq, and are now preserved in the Berlin Academy of Sciences; they have been published by F. Weller, who attributes them to a period around the sixth or the seventh century, and has shown them to be remains of a Sanskrit text more ancient than any preserved in the Nepalese tradition.[2] It is precisely the *Buddha-carita* which, in our view, provides so many points of contact with the Barlaam and Ioasaph story.

Now the Turfan expeditions, as is well known, brought back a great quantity of Manichaean documents and fragments in

[1] F. C. Burkitt, *The Religion of the Manichees*, Cambridge, 1925, pp. 44-5.
[2] See *Abhandlungen der Sächsischen Akademie der Wissenschaften, Phil.-hist. Klasse*, Band XLVI, Heft 4, Berlin, 1953.

Soghdian and Old Turkish. For the most part, the Turkish texts are translations from an Iranian original. The demand for them arose largely in connection with a Uigur *qaghan* or emperor's conversion to Manichaeism, commemorated by the edict of 762; in the tenth century, the Arabic bibliographer Ibn al-Nadīm reported that Manichaeism was protected by the Turks of Toquz Oghuz, 'The Nine Clans', living in Chinese Turkestan, east of Kashgar; while al-Bīrūnī, writing about A.D. 1000, said with some exaggeration that 'most of the eastern Turks, of the people of China and Tibet, and some of the Hindus, adhere to Mani's law and doctrine.'[1]

Two of the Old Turkish fragments bear directly on the question of the formation of the Barlaam and Ioasaph romance. The first of these, published by A. von Le Coq in the *Sitzungsberichte* of the Berlin Academy for 1909, is entitled: 'Book of the information given by Chinak (Chandaka) to the Bodisav (Bodhisattva) Prince'. With emendations suggested by W. Bang in *Le Muséon* (1931), the text in question reads as follows:

'... Thereupon the Bodisav Prince drew in the reins of his horse Kaṇṭhaka (?) and halted. Gazing, he asked Chinak: That creature lying there so hideous and grovelling, what sort of man is he? Chinak replied, saying respectfully: Your Highness, that man was once a young, healthy, slim, fair youth like yourself. Now he has become old and sick; and since he is afflicted with infirmity, he lies in so hideous a condition! Then the Bodisav spoke thus: Shall we also after a long life finally become dust like this? ... (4 lines missing) ... When the Bodisav Prince had heard this account from Chinak, he caught up the reins and returned home in bitter grief and great sorrow. He rode home into his city and spoke not a word to anyone; disconsolate still he sat down there. When his father the king and his mother the queen heard of this, they both came along; but whatever they might say to their son, he returned no answer. Then King Satudan (? Shantudan) said sternly to his officers and dignitaries: Follow him along every street, and let horns be blown in the hearing of all the nation. ...

Now this, of course, is one of the Four Omens or Encounters, after which it had been predicted that the Bodhisattva Prince would forsake the world. This episode is prominent in all the

---

[1] *Chronology of the Ancient Nations*, trans. Sachau, p. 191.

European versions of the Barlaam and Ioasaph romance, as well as in the intermediate Oriental recensions, including the Georgian *Wisdom of Balahvar*. The proper names are still recognizable as belonging to the Sanskrit tradition: Chinak is the Buddha's faithful charioteer Chandaka, while Satudan is Gautama's father, Śuddhodana. The form Bodisav for the hero's name is important: on the one hand, it renders the title Bodhisattva, while foreshadowing the next stage in transmission, the Arabic Būdhāsaf.

Another pointer to the existence of a Manichaean prototype of the Barlaam and Ioasaph story is provided by the second Turfan fragment which concerns us here, namely a Manichaean Turkish version of an unsavoury tale which later occurs in the Arabic adaptation of the work by Ibn Bābūya.[1] This relates how a certain prince becomes so intoxicated that he falls into a grave and mistakes a corpse for a desirable maiden. When he awakes he is horrified at his own conduct. This is obviously a lurid illustration of the Manichaean aversion to sexual pleasure; the anecdote is omitted from all the Christian recensions.

It is also interesting to note that a possible allusion to a form of the Barlaam and Ioasaph legend occurs in a Manichaean liturgical book written in Soghdian and Parthian, and also recovered by the Turfan expeditions. This devotional manual lays down as prescribed reading a parable from a work called 'The Prince with the Chandā[..]'s son'. While it is not quite clear from the defective manuscript whether one is to read 'Son of Chandaka', i.e. of Buddha's charioteer, or 'Son of a Chaṇḍāla', i.e. an outcast or untouchable, yet it is highly tempting to connect this brief allusion with the Barlaam and Ioasaph legend.[2]

At all events, the early Arabic authorities certainly associated Budhasaf, the Buddha-elect, with an Iranian and a Manichaean environment. How else is one to account for the odd affirmation by al-Mas'ūdī to the effect that Budhasaf was the founder of the Sabaean religion as professed in Harran, while another sect inhabited Iraq, between Wāsiṭ and Basra—precisely the environment in which Mani was brought up? Elaborating on this same theme, al-Bīrūnī represents Budhasaf as having brought into use the Iranian alphabet![3]

---

[1] S. von Oldenburg, in the *Izvestiya* of the Imperial Academy of Sciences, St. Petersburg, 6th series, VI, 1912, 779-82.
[2] W. B. Henning, *Ein manichäisches Bet- und Beichtbuch*, Berlin, 1936-7, pp. 46-7, 99.
[3] References given by P. Alfaric in *Journal Asiatique*, 1917, pp. 286-7.

One Arabic theologian regarded Budhasaf, the Bodhisattva, as suitable for condemnation along with Zoroaster, the Gnostics and the Manichaeans. In a work on Muslim schisms and sects, *Al-farq bain al-firaq*, by Abū-Manṣūr 'Abd-al-Qāhir ibn Ṭāhir al-Baghdādī (d. A.D. 1037), a list of false prophets occurs in the third chapter, which is 'an exposition of the fundamental dogma upon which the Orthodox are in mutual agreement'. Here it is stated that 'they approve of considering a heretic everyone who falsely claims to be a prophet, whether he lived before the days of Islam, like Zarādusht, Yūdāsaf, Mānī, Bardaisan, Marcion and Mazdak ... and the others after them who falsely claimed prophecy', and so forth.[1] Note that this author, through confusion of diacritical points in Arabic script, writes Yūdāsaf in place of Būdhāsaf. This form, from which first the Georgian Iodasaph, and then the Greek Ioasaph derive, is fairly common among the Arabic authorities.

As will be shown in the following chapter, the Barlaam and Ioasaph legend next makes its appearance in eighth century Baghdad. To account for its transmission thither from India and Central Asia, it has been suggested that there existed an intermediate Zoroastrian Pehlevi version. But the mood of disgust with earthly existence characteristic of our story is quite alien to the Zoroastrian view of life. Furthermore, the Manichees for centuries were active in both Central Asia and in Mesopotamia. In the late tenth century, Ibn al-Nadīm says that he knew of three hundred secret Manichees in Baghdad alone, while the faith of Mani was still tolerated in Samarkand. From the evidence before us, it seems clear that there was ample time and opportunity between the death of Mani in the third century and the appearance of the Arabic version in the eighth for the story of Budhasaf, the Bodhisattva, to take shape among the Manichaeans of Central Asia and be transmitted in an Iranian tongue to their co-religionists in Mesopotamia.

---

[1] Translated by A. S. Halkin, Tel-Aviv, 1935, pp. 200-1.

CHAPTER III

THE ARABIC VERSIONS

Trade relations had early brought the Arabs into contact with peoples who professed the Buddhist faith. In the first phases of Islam, the Muslim conquerors overran many territories which were or had been dominated by Buddhism. References to Buddhist temples and monks occur in early Islamic historical literature, even allowing for occasional confusion with Brahmanism. However, such writers as Shahrastānī give a coherent if laconic account of the tenets of the Buddhist religion, and show awareness of the differences which separate it from other Eastern faiths. Adapting, like the Classical writers before them, the Indian term *samaṇa*, usually used to designate a Buddhist ascetic, some of the Arabic authorities refer to the Buddha as the prophet of *samaniyya*.[1]

The late Ignaz Goldziher devoted much study to the influence of Buddhism on Muslim theology, publishing a special monograph on this theme, written in Hungarian, the substance of which is incorporated in his *Vorlesungen über den Islam*. In this scholar's view, 'the religious conception which stands out in opposition to orthodox Islam and is termed *zuhd* or asceticism, and is not identical with Ṣūfism, shows strong traces of the penetration of Indian ideals of life.' In a couplet by Abu' l-'Atāhiya (A.D. 748-828):—

If thou would'st see the noblest of mankind,
Behold a monarch in a beggar's garb,

an echo has been discerned of the story of the Buddha.[2] Parallels have also been drawn between the Ṣūfī and the Buddhist ideals of renunciation and self-abnegation. As in Buddhism the adept rises step by step along eight stages of the Noble Way towards the annihilation of the individual personality, so Ṣūfism too has its *ṭarīqa* or Way, marked by various stages of progress towards perfection, those proceeding along that way being known

---

[1] For elucidation of this term, I am indebted to Professor J. Brough and Professor A. S. Tritton.
[2] Compare R. A. Nicholson, *A Literary History of the Arabs*, revised ed., Cambridge, 1941, p. 298. Goldziher's evidence is summarized in a review-article by T. Duka in the *Journal of the Royal Asiatic Society*, 1904.

as *al-sālikūna*, 'those who walk'. The biography of an early saint of Ṣūfism, Ibrāhīm b. Adham (d. about A.D. 777), contains traits reminiscent of the legend of the Buddha-elect. Ibrāhīm, a royal prince of Balkh, is in one version represented as receiving a divine summons; in another, he is portrayed as watching from his palace window the hard life of a poor man outside, after which he throws off his royal cloak and exchanges it for beggar's rags, gives up all connection with the world, leaves the palace with his wife and children there, departs into the wilderness and leads a wandering life. The biography of Ibrāhīm b. Adham by Jalāl al-Dīn Rūmī contains a picturesque trait: One night the prince's guards heard noises on the palace roof, and found there some men who asserted that they were looking for their camels which had got loose and run away. The prince enquired of the intruders: 'Whoever has found camels on the roof of a house?' To which they replied: 'We are but following your example, for while seated on a throne, you still entertain hopes of coming nigh to God. In such a posture, who has ever been able to approach Him?' This retort determined Ibrāhīm b. Adham to renounce earthly glory.

Indeed, the motif of rulers casting off their pomp for a life of austerity, recalling the life of Gautama Buddha, is quite familiar in Islamic literature. In another such tale cited by Goldziher, a monarch one day catches sight of two grey hairs in his beard. He plucks these out, but they grow again every time. This makes him reflect: 'These are two envoys sent to me by God to warn me to forsake the world and devote myself to Him. So I will obey them.' Forthwith, he leaves his realm and wanders amidst the forest and desert places until his death. This, of course, is simply an adaptation of the familiar tale of King Makhādeva's grey hairs, from the Jātaka stories.[1]

Now the 'Abbasid caliphs who ruled from A.D. 750 onwards gave a new orientation to Islamic culture. The capital was moved from Damascus to Baghdad, which, founded in 762, rapidly became a highly cosmopolitan centre. Persian and, through its intermediary, Indian literature became popular, symptomatic of this being the vogue enjoyed by the Arabic translation of *Kalila wa Dimna*, which derives via the Pehlevi from the Indian *Pancatantra*, better known in Europe as the *Fables of Bidpai*. The translator, a Persian named Ibn al-Muqaffaʻ Rūzbeh, made a number of other renderings from the Iranian, before being executed by

[1] H. T. Francis and E. J. Thomas, *Jātaka Tales*, Cambridge, 1916, pp. 18-20.

the Caliph Manṣūr for suspected heresy in or about the year 759.

According to orthodox Arabic authorities, the reign of Manṣūr's son Mahdī (775-85) was marked by an upsurge not only of Iranian cultural influences generally, but of Manichaean propaganda in particular. Mas'ūdī complains that under Mahdī, 'religious heresies appeared and took root following the publication of the works of Mani, Bardaisan and Marcion, translated from the Parsi and Pehlevi into Arabic by 'Abdullāh Ibn al-Muqaffa' and other scholars. At the same time there appeared books by ... the continuators of the Manichaean, Daisanite and Marcionite sects. Atheism made its appearance and was swiftly propagated.'[1]

It is against this background that one must examine the information on the Arabic versions of the life of Buddha which is given in the bibliographical treatise, *Kitāb al-Fihrist*, composed by Muḥammad Ibn al-Nadīm al-Baghdādī in A.D. 987-8 and edited in the last century by G. Flügel. From this work we learn that among the books translated from Pehlevi into Arabic towards the second half of the second century of the Hijra (i.e. about A.D. 767 to 815) were a *Kitāb al-Budd*, or 'Book of the Buddha'; a *Kitāb Balauhar wa Būdhāsaf*, or 'Book of Balauhar and Budhasaf'; and a *Kitāb Būdhāsaf mufrad*, or 'Book of Budhasaf by himself'.

While it is doubtful whether they retain their original form completely, all three of these works have come down to us. The second title, as we shall see, is the one which directly concerns the transmission of the Barlaam and Ioasaph story.

The *Kitāb al-Budd* was merged in course of time with the *Kitāb Balauhar wa Būdhāsaf*, and appears in the form of episodes grafted on to the latter work in the Bombay edition of 1888/9, of which more presently. It is quite easy to distinguish the sections which really belong to the *Kitāb al-Budd*, because the Arabic adapter failed to realise that al-Budd and Budhasaf were in this instance one and the same person. Thus, passages in which al-Budd appears can safely be isolated from the rest of the book. These include a number of extremely curious fables and tales, in one of which the 'Anqā' bird, or Phoenix, is made to feed its offspring on the Buddha's corpse.

The *Kitāb Būdhāsaf mufrad* or 'Book of Budhasaf by himself' has survived as a chapter in an Arabic work called *Nihāyat al-arab fī akhbār al-Furs wa'l-'Arab*, which deals among other subjects with the legendary history of the ancient Persian kings. The chapter

[1] See the references given by Alfaric, *Les écritures manichéennes*, I, 75-8.

on the Budhasaf Prince, which the manuscripts at Cambridge and in the British Museum attribute to Ibn al-Muqaffaʻ, was summarized by Professor E. G. Browne, and later published and translated by Baron V. Rosen.[1] In brief, the story tells of a certain King Farrukhān, appointed by Alexander the Great to reign in Old Nihavand in Iran. As Farrukhān had no son, he and all his subjects were afraid that the dynasty would be extinguished. In response to their prayers, a son was born to the royal pair, who named him Budhasaf. When the prince grew up, he assimilated every branch of knowledge, and began to reflect on 'the fragility of the blessings granted by this world to those that dwell therein, on their many bereavements and tribulations, and on the excessive toil and burden of worries which fall to the lot of anyone who becomes involved therewith, and how all this leads eventually to eternal torments. And his spirit yearned towards renunciation and forsaking of this world.'

The Budhasaf Prince tells his father, King Farrukhān, of his aspirations. The king tries to dissuade him from forsaking his royal estate, on the grounds that he must first satisfy his creditors, namely, the subjects whom he is proposing to deprive of the just rule he owes them and on which they had been counting. Farrukhān proposes to hold a debate, in which Simeon the Monk is to act as arbiter. From this debate, the Budhasaf Prince emerges victorious with Simeon's assistance, and then takes leave of his father and dons hermit's attire to lead a wandering life.

Eventually, Budhasaf arrives in the neighbourhood of Ahwaz in Khuzistan on the borders of Iraq, where he builds a hermitage for himself and leads the life of a recluse. He encounters the king of Ahwaz, with whom he has a discussion in which the vanity of earthly glory is contrasted with the glorious prospect of the soul's salvation. The daughter of the king of Ahwaz is fired with the ambition to join Budhasaf in his pious way of life, and he accepts her as his wife: their union is not at first physically consummated, but consists in joint prayers to God.

Later, ambassadors come from Old Nihavand to announce the death of King Farrukhān and to take Budhasaf home to be their sovereign. He refuses to go, and they refer the matter to a hermit whose name is given as Mar-Ḍevāriāh (?). At length, Budhasaf and his wife consent to return and assume royal power. Their

[1] See *J. R. A. S.*, 1900, pp. 216-7; *Zapiski* of the Oriental Section of the Imperial Russian Archaeological Society, XIV, St. Petersburg, 1901-2, pp. 77-118.

union is consummated, and they produce a son, Adharwān, who later succeeds his father and reigns until the local dynasts of Iran are exterminated by Ardashir.

The tale is embellished with a series of fables, though none of these correspond to those included in the Barlaam and Ioasaph romance. Thus, the 'Book of Budhasaf by himself' is seen to be an independent offshoot of the story of the Buddha-elect, transplanted from its Indian background into an Iranian context.

It now falls to discuss the Arabic work which mainly concerns us, namely the *Kitāb Balauhar wa Būdhāsaf*. That this was in circulation about the year A.D. 800 is confirmed by further particulars given by Ibn al-Nadīm in the *Fihrist*, according to which (p. 119) the book of Balauhar and Budhasaf was versified by the Baghdad poet Abān al-Lāḥiqī, who died in the year 200 of the Hijra, or A.D. 815/6. This Abān was a well-known literary figure of the time of Harun al-Rashid, whose protégé he was. He also turned into verse the *Kalīla wa Dimna* and the Book of Sindbad, and composed a work on the Wisdom of the Hindus. In view of what has been said about the Manichaean fragments of the Budhasaf or Bodhisattva story, it is of interest to note that Abān was himself accused of being a *zindīq*, a term deriving from *zaddīq*, which means a member of the Manichee Elect, but was later adapted to designate anyone suspected of heretical or atheistic leanings. It does not appear, however, that Abān came to grief; officially, he remained a member of the Muslim confession. His metrical version of the story of Balauhar and Budhasaf has not come down to us. An interesting biography of Abān al-Lāḥiqī by A. E. Krymsky, with a study of the Arabic and other versions of the Barlaam romance, was published at Moscow in 1913.

The earliest surviving version of the Arabic Balauhar and Budhasaf (Barlaam and Ioasaph) story to which a more or less precise date can be assigned is an adaptation incorporated in a tenth century work on the Shī'a doctrine of the Hidden Imam. This treatise, known as the 'Book of the Perfection of Faith and the Accomplishment of Felicity' (*Kitāb ikmāl al-dīn wa'itmām al-ni'ma*), was composed by Ibn Bābūya of Qum, an important theological writer who worked for a time in Baghdad and died at Rayy in Persia in A.D. 991. There is no reason to doubt that he had at his disposal one of the very earliest Arabic translations of the Balauhar and Budhasaf story, though he treats the second portion of the work in an independent manner. The Ibn Bābūya version is important as containing the unsavoury tale of the drunken prince and the dead body, which has been noted as occurring in one of the Turfan Manichaean fragments. The original Arabic text of Ibn Bābūya's treatise is listed by Ahlwardt as No. 2721 of the Berlin collection, while two copies of a seventeenth century Persian translation feature in Rieu's supplementary catalogue of the Persian manuscripts in the British Museum, Nos. 36 and 380. An analysis of the portion dealing with Balauhar and Budhasaf, with copious extracts from the text, is given by S. von Oldenburg in the *Zapiski* of the Oriental Section of the Imperial Russian Archaeological Society, volume IV (1890), pages 229-65.

Somewhat akin to Ibn Bābūya's version of the Balauhar and Budhasaf legend is the defective Arabic text contained in a manuscript belonging to the German Oriental Society's library in Halle and copied in A.H. 1099/1688 A.D. This recension, published at Vienna in 1888 by F. Hommel in the Proceedings of the 7th International Congress of Orientalists, states itself to be 'an abridgement from the book of one of the distinguished philosophers of India'.[1] By comparison with the Bombay and Ibn Bābūya versions, the Halle abstract contains little local colour, and is much shortened; most of the personal and geographical names are omitted, Budhasaf, the Bodhisattva, not being given any designation beyond that of 'the king's son'. This Halle text is incomplete, breaking off at the point where the king, Budhasaf's father, is concerting measures with a sorcerer to turn the prince away from his new-found ideals and make him revert to idolatry. Discrepancies between the Halle and Ibn Bābūya versions make it clear that neither derives from the other, but that both go back to a common source, no doubt the *Kitāb Balauhar wa Būdhāsaf* mentioned in the *Fihrist*.

By far the most complete extant text of the Arabic story of Balauhar and Budhasaf is contained in a book published by Shaykh Nūr al-Dīn ibn Jīwākhān at the Ṣafdarian Printing Press, Bombay in A.H. 1306/1888-9 A.D., under the title, 'Book of Balauhar and Budhasaf, with Exhortations and Parables filled with Wisdom'. As already mentioned, this is a composite work containing more or less authentic versions of two of the stories of Buddha listed in the *Fihrist*, namely the *Kitāb Balauhar wa Būdhāsaf* and the *Kitāb al-Budd*. It is this Bombay Arabic edition which contains the largest

[1] English translation by E. Rehatsek, 'Book of the King's Son and the Ascetic', *J. R. A. S.*, 1890, pp. 119-55.

number of parables and anecdotes, over forty in all, though many of these do not belong to the story of Balauhar and Budhasaf, but to that of al-Budd. The researches of Kuhn, Chauvin, Jacobs and others have produced Indian parallels for many of the fables occurring in Balauhar's homilies, though surprisingly few of these parallels are with stories of a specifically Buddhist character. The parable of the Sower, on the other hand, is clearly taken from the New Testament. The eclectic method by which Balauhar's parables seem to have been assembled may lend further support to the idea of an earlier Manichaean redaction.

A feature of all the Arabic versions is the strictly limited extent to which they have been coloured by Islamic doctrine. The precise nature of the ascetic faith to which the Budhasaf/Bodhisattva prince is called is left vague, being referred to as 'the true religion' or by some such general designation. The name of Muḥammad the Prophet occurs only in a few conventional pious formulae scattered here and there by a redactor or scribe.

This does not mean, however, that the story of Balauhar and Budhasaf made no impression on Islamic thinkers and theologians. A twice repeated allusion to our tale, as to a book of wide circulation and standard authority, occurs in the encyclopaedic work called *Rasā'il Ikhwān al-Ṣafā'*, or 'Philosophical Treatises of the Brothers of Purity'. According to a thirteenth century authority cited by R. A. Nicholson, the Brothers of Purity flourished at Basra towards the end of the tenth century. 'They formed a society for the pursuit of holiness, purity and truth, and established amongst themselves a doctrine whereby they hoped to win the approval of God, maintaining that the Religious Law was defiled by ignorance and adulterated by errors, and that there was no means of cleansing and purifying it except philosophy, which united the wisdom of faith and the profit of research. They held that a perfect result would be reached if Greek philosophy were combined with Arabian religion. Accordingly they composed fifty tracts on every branch of philosophy, theoretical as well as practical, added a separate index, and entitled them the "Tracts of the Brethren of Purity". The authors of this work concealed their names, but circulated it among the booksellers and gave it to the public. They filled their pages with devout phraseology, religious parables, metaphorical expressions, and figurative turns of style.'[1]

---
[1] *Literary History of the Arabs*, p. 370.

From internal evidence, it appears that the authors of the *Rasā'il* combined ultra-Shī'ī convictions with a sort of idealistic pantheism. Some have seen in these treatises a vehicle for Ismā'īlī propaganda. The system of universal fellowship preached by the Brothers of Purity certainly has revolutionary and incendiary aspects, though it is not clear whether they constituted a regular political organization. 'Ours,' they declared, 'is a catholic and universal system, which absorbs in itself all systems of religion.' The professed aim of the fraternity was the salvation of men's immortal souls by mutual assistance and purifying knowledge. With this in view, they strove to find 'a teacher who is broad-minded, a friend of knowledge, a seeker of truth'. Their metaphysics was based on the idea that the world derived from God by emanation. They believed in the heavenly origin of the soul and its ultimate return to God. The individual human soul is visualized as part of the world soul. Thus, the death of the individual is called the minor resurrection, and the return of the world soul to its Creator, the major resurrection. Within this framework, the teachings of the Brothers of Purity are eclectic, being culled in large part from a number of philosophical writings current in the eighth and ninth centuries. Thus, a neo-Platonist tendency has been traced in the *Rasā'il*, and there are references to Hermes, Pythagoras and Socrates. The Brothers were also versed in the lore of Iran and of India, as transmitted through such works as the *Kalīla wa Dimna*.

The first of two references to the 'Book of Balauhar and Budhasaf' in the 'Philosophical Treatises of the Brothers of Purity' (Cairo edition, 1928, IV, pp. 120 and 223) occurs in a discussion of immortality and the hereafter; it follows an allusion to the words of Socrates on taking the hemlock and preparing for his death. The authors of the *Rasā'il* then refer to Balauhar's conversation with Budhasaf (given here in the form Yūzāsaf) in connection with an enquiry addressed by a king to his vazir relating to 'those people who had knowledge of the kingdom of heaven'. The second mention of Balauhar and Budhasaf in the tracts in question is merely a briefer repetition of the first, with the remark that a discourse on the hereafter would be found in the 'Book of Balauhar and Budhasaf'.

There can be no doubt that the reference here is to Balauhar's parable of the King, the Righteous Vazir and the Happy Poor Couple, in which a monarch observes two ragged paupers living merrily in a cave hollowed out of a garbage mound and is led to contrast their way of life favourably with his own. In the Halle Arabic version (compare Rehatsek's translation, pp. 145-6), the vazir draws the moral that 'to those who know the everlasting kingdom, a monarchy is as this locality appears to our eyes; and to those who hope for the mansions of eternal beatitude, thy mansions will appear as this cave appears to our eyes.'

The king then asks: 'And who are the people of this description, and what do they describe concerning the everlasting kingdom?'

The vazir answers: 'They are those who know God and seek eternity, namely the mansion of joy wherewith grief neither exists nor follows it, but rather repose not fraught with fatigue, and light which is not followed by darkness, and knowledge not commingled with ignorance, and love not accompanied by hate; and content and security, neither of which is coupled with wrath nor fear, and whatever is beautiful or pleasant, without any admixture of baseness or decay in either; health and life, followed neither by sickness nor by death, perfect immunity from all evils, and the plenitude of everything good.'

This eloquent passage is reproduced in a Christian context in both Georgian versions, *The Life of the Blessed Iodasaph* in the Jerusalem manuscript, and *The Wisdom of Balahvar* translated in this volume; it found its way with only slight modification into the Greek Barlaam and Ioasaph romance (Loeb edition, pp. 232-3) and thence into the Western European versions. The fact that the story of Budhasaf, the Bodhisattva, was consulted and recommended by the Brothers of Purity is interesting evidence of its wide appeal.

While discussing the Arabic versions, mention should also be made of the Hebrew metrical rendering, *The King's Son and the Ascetic*, by the Spanish rabbi Abraham bar Samuel Halevi ibn Chisdai, who died about 1220. Since Ibn Chisdai gives several fables found in the early Arabic texts of the 'Book of Balauhar and Budhasaf', but absent from the Christian Barlaam and Ioasaph romance, he must have made his rendering from an early Arabic version; he adds several fables of his own. Ibn Chisdai's work has been translated into German; a detailed study of the text was published by N. Weisslowits in 1890.

In conclusion, it may be useful to list the principal personal and geographical names found in the Barlaam and Ioasaph romance, as they occur in the Arabic texts which, of course, precede all the Christian versions. It is important to bear these forms in mind when studying the filiation of the different redactions.

PERSONAL NAMES

1. Balauhar — An ascetic philosopher.
2. Būdhāsaf — An Indian king's son, later a disciple of Balauhar. Also found in the form Yūzāsaf, while Mas'ūdī has Yūdāsaf, as do certain other Arabic authorities.
3. Janaysar — A heathen king of India (cf. Sanskrit 'janeśvara', a king).
4. Rakis — An astrologer, Janaysar's confidant.
5. Al-Bahwan — An idol-worshipping ascetic. The name has also been read as al-Tahdam.

GEOGRAPHICAL NAMES

1. Serendīb — Arabic name for Ceylon, the abode of the ascetic Balauhar.
2. Shawilābaṭṭ — Centre of Janaysar's kingdom, corresponding to Kapilavastu; may also be read as Sūlābaṭ.

CHAPTER IV

THE GEORGIAN VERSIONS

Once it had been accepted that the Christian Greek version of the Barlaam and Ioasaph romance was connected with the non-Christian Arabic book of Balauhar and Budhasaf, scholars were faced with the problem of finding a link between the two. Several of those who concerned themselves in the last century with this question postulated that there must have existed a Syriac recension, now lost, to fill this role. As Joseph Jacobs put it, 'Syriac was the main conduit pipe through which the treasures of Greek literature debouched on to the Orient, and inversely, it was mainly through Syriac versions that Oriental treasures were added to Greco-Byzantine literature.' The late Nicholas Marr, who first made the Georgian *Wisdom of Balahvar* available for study, thought rather that this latter work was a translation from the Syriac, and that the Greek rendering was then made from the Georgian, thus providing for two (and not one) intermediate links between the Arabic and the Greek. But since researches in Syriac over the last century have failed to yield any version or direct trace of the Barlaam and Ioasaph romance in that language, it is more than doubtful whether a Syriac recension ever existed.

As an alternative, one would naturally look in Christian Arabic literature for the required intermediary; however, the Christian Arabic texts so far known to us are all later derivates from the Greek. The same applies to the Armenian adaptations, which include one in verse. Of even less value is the Ethiopic, which derives via the Christian Arabic from the Greek.

To the late Father Paul Peeters belongs the credit of having shown that there is no need to look for a Syriac intermediary, since the Georgian shows every sign of being a direct translation from the Arabic book of Balauhar and Budhasaf. At the same time, Peeters adduced fresh evidence to show that it was indeed the Georgian version which provided a basis for the more elaborate Greco-Byzantine romance of Barlaam and Ioasaph.[1]

[1] P. Peeters, 'La première traduction latine de "Barlaam et Joasaph" et son original grec', in *Analecta Bollandiana*, XLIX, 1931, pp. 276-312.

The Georgians, a martial people inhabiting the Caucasus, had adopted the Christian faith during the reign of Constantine the Great, about the year A.D. 330. After their conversion by the semi-legendary St. Nino, they were at first in communion with the Armenian Gregorian Church. Subsequently, after the schism at Chalcedon, the Georgians broke away. From the year 607 onwards, they adhered faithfully to Byzantine Greek Orthodoxy. The Georgian alphabet dates from the fifth century. From thenceforth, the Holy Scriptures and the devotional writings of the early Fathers were translated into Georgian, at first mainly from Armenian, and later from the Greek direct. Other works were translated from Syriac and Arabic.

For our present purpose, it is important to bear in mind that in addition to Georgia's Byzantine orientation, the country stood for centuries in close relationship with the Arab Caliphate. Within a generation of the death of Muḥammad the Prophet, Armenia and much of Transcaucasia up to the Caspian Sea had been overrun by the armies of Islam. Tiflis, the capital of Georgia, capitulated about the year 655, and was from then on governed by an Arab amir or viceroy under the directions of the caliphs of Damascus and, later, of Baghdad. Although the local Christians were generally tolerated, mosques were built in Tiflis and coins with Arabic inscriptions struck in the name of the caliph. The city was not recovered by the Christian Georgian kings until 1122; to the present day, it retains a strong Muslim element. All this resulted in the Georgians acquiring a veneer of Islamic culture, especially among the urban and upper classes of society. Some of the Christian Georgian nobles even adopted Arabic names and lived in close touch with the Saracen viceroys and their entourage. Georgian princes disobedient to the caliph's will were liable to be summoned to Baghdad and, if not executed, detained there under house arrest.

Conversely, a few of the Arabs resident in Georgia were converted to Christianity. The best known of these was St. Abo of Tiflis, martyred in 786. Abo was a perfumer from Baghdad who travelled to Georgia as a member of the staff of the ruling prince Nerses of Iberia. It is worth noting that Abo is described by his contemporary biographer, John Sabanisdze, as originally being 'versed in the literature of the Saracens', whereas later 'he learnt to read and write and converse freely in Georgian'.[1] This is

[1] Lang, *Lives and Legends of the Georgian Saints*, London, 1956, p. 117.

just the type of contact which could have resulted in the translation into Georgian of an Arabic text like the book of Balauhar and Budhasaf which, as already noted, was current in Baghdad precisely in Abo's time.

The Georgians' suitability for the role of middlemen in literary exchanges between the Muslim and Byzantine worlds was further enhanced by the number of monastic settlements which they possessed throughout the Near East. By the time of Justinian, in the sixth century, the Georgians and the Laz had two cloisters in the neighbourhood of Jerusalem. Before the eighth century, a school of Georgian monastic translators and copyists was established at the Lavra of St. Saba near Jerusalem, where they celebrated prayers in their native tongue and occupied special quarters called the Grotto of the Georgians. Monks from Georgia were also established in or near Jerusalem at the monasteries of St. Samuel, St. Simeon and St. Chariton, as well as on Mount Golgotha. From about 1038 or slightly earlier dates the foundation of the Monastery of the Holy Cross near Jerusalem by St. Prochorus the Georgian; the collection of manuscripts formerly belonging to that monastery is now in the Greek Patriarchal Library at Jerusalem.

Inscriptions lately discovered show further that the Georgians were established about the seventh century in a cloister at Bethlehem, dedicated to St. Theodore. On Mount Horeb, they had two churches. There was an active Georgian community in St. Catharine's monastery on Mount Sinai; of the large manuscript collection there, one Georgian codex is dated A.D. 864. In Syria, round about Antioch and notably on the Black Mountain, the Georgians had many hermitages: there were sixty Georgian monks at St. Simeon's monastery on Mons Admirabilis, and others at the cloisters of St. Romanus, St. Procopius, St. Barlaam of Mount Casios, St. Calliopius and Castana.[1] In and around such centres as these, the Georgians would come into contact with a Muhammadan population as well as with representatives of other Christian nations.

Within the Greco-Byzantine sphere of influence, the Georgians also occupied a number of monastic establishments. Thus, St. Hilarion the Iberian, who lived in the ninth century, travelled from his native land to Palestine, thence to Constantinople and to

---

[1] P. Peeters, *Le tréfonds oriental de l'hagiographie byzantine*, Brussels, 1950, pp. 160-3, 202-6.

Rome. After settling on Mount Olympus, he finally died in A.D. 875 at Thessalonica; so great was his pious fame that the Emperor Basil I founded the Romana Cloister near Constantinople as a shrine for Hilarion's relics. Three hermitages on Olympus were occupied at this period by Georgian holy men: the Cloister of the Holy Virgin, that of Saints Cosmas and Damian, and the Crania Lavra. From the year 980, the foundation of the Iviron or Georgian Monastery on Mount Athos by Saints John and Euthymius and their brethren gave a new impetus to Georgian monastic life within the Byzantine orbit. Even in the Balkans, Georgian religious zeal found an outlet: in 1083, the Petridsoni monastery was founded at Bachkovo in Bulgaria by Gregory Bakuriani, a high officer of Armeno-Georgian descent in the service of the Imperial court. In Cyprus too, groups of Georgian monks were settled at a cloister called 'Zhalia', or The Violet, as well as near Alamino.

Life in these monastic settlements was by no means always sedentary or static. The monks and abbots, as we read in their biographies, were often engaged in pilgrimages and missionary activity, and even acted as diplomatic representatives of the Georgian monarchy. Nor did they necessarily remain permanently attached to one foundation. Some would serve a novitiate within Georgia and then proceed to Jerusalem or Sinai, to Antioch or Mount Athos. Thus, liaison was maintained between Georgian monks within the Arab and the Greek dominions, while contacts with pilgrims kept them in touch with their homeland in the Caucasus.

It is against this background that we have to examine the part played by the Georgians in the transmission of the Barlaam and Ioasaph romance. It is important to remember that they were quite accustomed to translate direct from the Arabic. The names of two Georgian fathers, David and Stephen, have come down to us as translators from this language. They worked at Jerusalem; indeed, most Georgian translations from the Arabic are of Syro-Palestinian provenance. Among such texts are the autobiography of the pseudo-Dionysius the Areopagite; the narrative by Antiochus Strategus of the sack of Jerusalem by the Persians in A.D. 614; the autobiography of the martyr Antony Rawah; and the Passions of St. Romanus and St. Michael the Sabaite.[1]

To this list of works translated from Arabic into Georgian must now be added the book of Balauhar and Budhasaf. Since the dis-

---

[1] Peeters, *Le tréfonds oriental*, p. 210.

covery some seventy years ago of an Old Georgian Christian recension, *The Wisdom of Balahvar*, in which the proper names are close to the Arabic, while the Christian framework and the selection of parables anticipate the Greek, a number of scholars have defended the view that this Georgian text provides the link between the Oriental and the Western Christian versions. Among those who have held this view, with variations of detail, we may name Baron V. Rosen, N. Y. Marr, Paul Peeters, R. L. Wolff and Sirarpie Ter Nersesean. It is this Georgian text which is presented in the second part of the present volume.

It cannot be denied, however, that *The Wisdom of Balahvar* is much shorter than either the Arabic or the Greek versions. Furthermore, certain episodes are presented in a quite different light, or suppressed altogether, which caused some scholars to view the Georgian version with a sceptical eye. There are even a few instances where disjointed effects and lack of sequence led Marr to suppose that this was in fact an abridgement of an earlier and more complete rendering.

The discovery of the new Jerusalem Georgian text, *The Life of the Blessed Iodasaph*, shows Marr's conjecture to be fully justified. The codex in which it is contained, No. 140 of the former Holy Cross Monastery collection, was first described by the late Robert P. Blake. Now that the Library of Congress Photoduplication Service kindly makes microfilms of this collection available to scholars, it has become clear that this is not simply another copy of *The Wisdom of Balahvar*, but a far fuller and more ancient version, of which *The Wisdom of Balahvar* is a condensation.

According to Blake's catalogue, Manuscript No. 140 is written on paper of small format, 185 × 133 mm., in single column; out of the whole codex, *The Life of the Blessed Iodasaph* occupies 343 pages of about 110 words each, giving a total of around 38,000 words, or over double the length of *The Wisdom of Balahvar*. While Blake was disposed to ascribe the manuscript to the thirteenth or the fourteenth century, it contains colophons or memorials mentioning St. Prochorus and a certain Chita, both of whom are identifiable as historical personages of the eleventh. For reasons which the writer hopes to set out more fully in an article contributed to the volume of essays dedicated by the School of Oriental and African Studies, London, to Sir R. L. Turner, it seems that our codex was most probably copied between A.D. 1060-1070. It is not without interest that the Prochorus mentioned in this manuscript, who founded the Holy Cross Monastery, was a disciple of St. Euthymius the Athonite, who has been connected with the translation of the Barlaam romance from Georgian into Greek. The successor of St. Euthymius, George the Hagiorite, who was also Euthymius' biographer, encouraged Prochorus in his work and visited him in Jerusalem. Besides several other lives of saints, our Jerusalem Manuscript No. 140 has bound in at the end a liturgical text composed by St. Basil and translated by Euthymius into Georgian; it is written in the distinctive Athonite hand with bold flourishes, quite different from the square, plain handwriting of the main body of the text.

The new Georgian Barlaam version is divided into two portions, each with a separate title-heading. The first page is badly rubbed. However, it is possible to reconstruct the heading and opening phrases more or less satisfactorily. We read them: 'Life and Acts of the Blessed Iodasap', son of Abenes, king of the Indians; whom the Blessed Father Balahvar the Teacher converted. Grant us thy blessing, O father!—— There was a certain king of the land of India, in the place which they call Bolaiti. . . .'

Study of the proper names, the order of fables, the sequence of episodes, as well as textual parallels of a striking nature, give a strong impression that this new Life of the Blessed Iodasap' (or Iodasaph) is nothing but an adaptation of the Arabic book of Balauhar and Budhasaf, heavily rewritten in parts in order to advocate specifically Christian doctrines.

To begin with, this fact is betrayed by the personal and geographical names. The Georgian Balahvar is the Balauhar of the Arabic. Iodasaph comes from the Arabic Budhasaf via the alternative Arabic form Yudasaf which we actually found used by some of the Arab authorities. The astrologer Rak'is (or Rakhis), confidant of Iodasaph's father, corresponds to the Rākis who occupies the same role in the Arabic version. It does not require much alteration of diacritical points in Arabic script to get Bolaiti out of Sūlābaṭ. Lastly, and most significantly, we have to note the mention in this new Georgian text of Balahvar's ascetic retreat as being situated in Sarnadib. Now this is merely the Arabic Serendīb, or Ceylon, stated in the Arabic version to be the place of Balauhar's abode. The shorter Georgian *Wisdom of Balahvar* omits to specify where Balahvar lived, while the Greek alters the place entirely, and makes him come from Senaar, or Mesopotamia.

As already mentioned, the new *Life of the Blessed Iodasaph* is far more nearly of the same length as the Bombay Arabic and the Greek version than is the shorter Georgian text previously known. What is more, a number of episodes altered or distorted in the abridged version can be restored by reference to the longer recension, in which they correspond closely to, and occupy a position midway between the Arabic and the Greek. This is made clear from the very outset, in the account of the character of Iodasaph's father, King Janaysar. According to the Bombay Arabic text, Janaysar's thoughts and energy were exclusively directed towards earthly blessings, while he revelled in the intoxication of his own might, and was intolerant towards those who preached pious doctrine; the Greek likewise depicts the king, here called Abenner, as 'mighty in riches and power, victorious over his enemies, brave in warfare, vain of his splendid stature and comeliness of face, and boastful of worldly honours, that pass so soon away'. Now those who had compared the various versions, like my friend R. L. Wolff of Harvard University, had not failed to remark that the shorter Georgian *Wisdom of Balahvar* which is presented in this volume portrays the king in a much more favourable light, as 'a man of peace-loving and humble character, and extremely charitable to the poor'. There is none of this indulgent tone in the new Jerusalem manuscript. Here, Iodasaph's father Abenes is described as 'dread and fearsome above all men, a victor over his foes, bold, haughty and fine to look upon. . . . Captive was he in habit and mind to the desires and delights of this world and enslaved by his own wilfulness, etc.' There is no word here of Abenes being humble or charitable. Thus, from the beginning the new Georgian *Life of the Blessed Iodasaph* is seen to belong more closely to the main line of transmission.

In the treatment of early episodes in the story, the Jerusalem Georgian version adheres far more closely to both the Arabic and the Greek than does the shorter Georgian text. Significant is the passage where the king's favourite satrap becomes a recluse and preaches him a sermon on the advantages of an ascetic life. This incident, completely absent from the abridged *Wisdom of Balahvar*, occupies several folios in the new Jerusalem manuscript, where it follows the arguments advanced in the Arabic version, and foreshadows the line of reasoning used in the more sophisticated Greek text. Just after this, yet another member of the royal entourage, a virtuous senator, is in both Arabic and Greek versions smitten with the prevailing religious fever and falls into disgrace, but is saved by the good advice of a wounded philosopher. Now in the short Georgian text, this senator is Balahvar himself, Iodasaph's future mentor. This ingenious twist to the original narrative makes it possible for the senator to retire into the wilderness and subsequently find his way back as a hermit to convert the young prince. This, however, is quite at variance with both the Arabic and the Greek accounts of the incident, where the virtuous senator has nothing whatever to do with Balahvar (Balauhar, Barlaam). That fact was early pointed out by Kuhn and others who fastened on to the discrepancies between the short Georgian and the other recensions. The new Jerusalem text now before us settles this difficulty; here, the virtuous senator or counsellor also has nothing to do with Balahvar, who appears without previous warning from his desert retreat in Sarnadib (Serendīb, this is, Ceylon).

The detailed comparison of the two Georgian texts which has been made by the present writer leaves no doubt that *The Wisdom of Balahvar* is in fact an abridgement of the new Jerusalem *Life of the Blessed Iodasaph*. The shorter version was intended for inclusion in collections of lives of the Saints and Church Fathers. After all, the Halle Arabic is similarly condensed from the 'Book of Balauhar and Budhasaf', while mediaeval Christian anthologists like Jacobus de Voragine had no scruples about chopping off the lengthy homilies of Barlaam and producing a short text for inclusion in such anthologies as the *Legenda Aurea*. This is exactly what happened to the Georgian version, which is further confirmed by the fact that the oldest manuscripts of the shorter *Wisdom of Balahvar* actually occur in volumes containing a selection of lives of Saints, such as the important manuscript No. 36 of this same Jerusalem collection.

If the editor who originally made the Georgian abridgement acted on the whole with remarkable ingenuity and some originality, he was not exempt from a few slips which further betray his activity. There is one incident in the middle of the story where the king and his astrologer Rakhis are trying to hunt down Balahvar (Barlaam) and put him to the torture. In the Arabic and the Greek versions, they manage to capture some other holy men, and both narratives add that 'their leader and captain bore a wallet of hair, charged with the relics of some holy Fathers departed this life'. (We quote from Woodward and Mattingly's translation of the Greek Barlaam in the Loeb edition, page 329; the Bombay Arabic is much to the same effect.) This leader of the hermit band acts as their spokesman in the ensuing argument with Rākis (Araches).

In the Georgian abridged version, *The Wisdom of Balahvar*, on the other hand, we are first told rather casually that all these hermits bore holy relics hanging at their necks, with no mention of any captain or leader of the band acting as spokesman; yet a few lines later, one finds a single hermit holding forth without any form of introduction beyond the words: 'And the man said. . . .'

This apparent inconsistency is cleared up by the new and fuller Jerusalem text, where one hermit is singled out as bearing the relics and sustaining the conversation with Rakhis all by himself, as in the Arabic and Greek versions. Whoever prepared the Georgian abridgement thus started by describing all the hermits rather loosely as bearing relics and arguing with Rakhis, omitting to specify that they had a leader and spokesman as stated in the longer version he was using as his model. A few lines later, he forgot that no single, individual speaker had been designated and simply inserted the exchange between the chief hermit and the pursuers more or less verbatim, producing a disjointed effect. (This is one of the few instances where inconsistencies in the shorter *Wisdom of Balahvar* have been rectified in the present translation by reference to the new Jerusalem text.)

To judge by the rather sketchy manner in which the concluding episodes of the shorter Georgian *Wisdom of Balahvar* are treated, one might conclude that the abridger had by this time wearied of his task. Iodasaph's farewell exhortation to his successor Barakhia, for instance, occupies scarcely two hundred words here; the jerky and abrupt effect which it produces caused Marr to remark that it failed to inspire confidence, and must be merely an extract from a more authentic and complete version since lost.[1] Now in the new Jerusalem text, *The Life of the Blessed Iodasaph*, this farewell exhortation occupies no less than twelve pages (folios 163r.-169r.). Comparison of the longer and shorter Georgian versions shows conclusively that, as Marr surmised, the exhortation in the shorter text consists merely of snippets extracted from the discourse in the longer recension, and rather carelessly threaded together without much regard for literary effect.

The same applies to the way in which Iodasaph's reunion with

---

[1] N.Y. Marr, 'Armyansko-gruzinskie materialy dlya istorii Dushepoleznoy Povesti o Varlaame i Ioasafe', in *Zapiski* of the Oriental Section of the Imperial Russian Archaeological Society, XI, 1897-8, p. 55.

Balahvar is dealt with. In the newly discovered Jerusalem text, Iodasaph goes to Sarnadib (Ceylon) and catches sight from afar of someone on a mountain wearing the hair garment which he had given to Balahvar when they had earlier exchanged clothes in token of Iodasaph's conversion. This clue leads to the reunion of the two holy men. In the shorter *Wisdom of Balahvar*, this episode is garbled beyond recognition, especially as some puzzled scribe has substituted at the crucial point the words *ert'sa mat't'agansa* ('on one of them') for *ert'sa shina mt'at'agan* ('on one of the mountains'). Here also, it has been felt to be justifiable to rectify this lapse when rendering the shorter Georgian version into English.

Contrary to the view of two eminent Tiflis scholars, S. Qaukhchishvili and Shalva Nutsubidze, *The Wisdom of Balahvar* must be recognized as an abridged adaptation of the longer Jerusalem text. Originally intended for purposes of edification, it has since been taken over into Georgian popular literature. The language of *The Wisdom of Balahvar* is certainly archaic, and bears strong affinities to the oldest version of the Georgian Gospels as preserved in the Adysh Codex copied in A.D. 897. To avoid wearying the reader, it will here suffice to refer to Father M. Tarchnišvili's survey of Georgian ecclesiastical literature, where this point is fully analysed.[1] Now since the prototype from which the Georgian renderings derive, namely the Arabic *Book of Balauhar and Budhasaf*, was current in Baghdad towards the end of the eighth century A.D., we shall not be far from the mark if we conclude that the story was first adapted in Georgian as a Christian morality between the years 800 and 900 after Christ.

To illustrate the conclusions reached through study of the new Jerusalem manuscript, namely that this Georgian *Life of the Blessed Iodasaph* is a direct adaptation of the Arabic story of the Bodhisattva in a Christian context, and thus lies at the base of all the Christian versions of the Barlaam and Ioasaph romance, there follows below an extended summary of the manuscript with references to corresponding passages of the Arabic and Greek recensions. For the Arabic, Baron V. Rosen's Russian translation of the Bombay edition, published under the editorship of the late Professor I. Krachkovsky in 1947, has been used; for the Greek, Woodward and Mattingly's edition and translation in the Loeb Classical Library. Special interest attaches to the fact that three

---

[1] M. Tarchnišvili, *Geschichte der kirchlichen georgischen Literatur*, Vatican City, 1955, pp. 395-6.

of the fables in the new Georgian version, 'Dogs and Carrion', 'Physician and Patient' and 'The Amorous Wife', are also found in the Arabic, but are absent from the Greek. The first two are also omitted from *The Wisdom of Balahvar*, as is the parable of 'The Sun'. (An English translation of these three parables is given at the end of this volume.) Thus, the Georgian *Life of the Blessed Iodasaph* has a fuller series of fables and parables than any other Christian version of the Barlaam romance.

*Summary of the Life of the Blessed Iodasaph
from manuscript No. 140 of the Jerusalem collection*

I

Once there reigned in India, at a place called Bolaiti, a great and powerful pagan king called Abenes. His only sorrow was that he was childless and so had no heir to whom he might bequeath his realm. He was hostile to the Christian faith and persecuted its adherents.

(Jerusalem Georgian text, fols. 1-2; Bombay Arabic, in Rosen's translation, pp. 23-4; Greek Barlaam, ed. and trans. Woodward and Mattingly, pp. 3-15.)

II

King Abenes heard that one of his chief men had been converted to the true faith, and had renounced the world to join the community of the ascetics. He summoned the sage, who preached the monarch a sermon on the vanity of the world and its pleasures. Abenes refused to pay heed to his arguments, and angrily ejected him from the realm.

(Jerusalem Georgian, fols. 3-10r.; Bombay Arabic, 24-31; Greek Barlaam, pp. 15-31.)

III

At last a son is born to the king, who names him Iodasaph. The astrologers declare that he will attain great honour and power, all except for one seer, the wisest of them all, who predicts that the child will renounce earthly pomp and become a prophet of the true faith. This upsets the king, who builds a city apart and keeps his son there, so that he may never know the real condition and fate of mankind.

(Jerusalem Georgian, fols. 10v.-11v.; Bombay Arabic, p. 31; Greek Barlaam, pp. 31-5.)

IV

Another member of the king's entourage, one of his ministers or senators, is also seized with pious zeal. He incurs the royal displeasure, but a maimed philosopher or 'patcher of words' whom he befriends shows him how to escape punishment. The king vents his anger on some holy monks who have delayed their departure from his realm. He burns many Christians in his wrath, after which cremation became an established custom in India. Here, the Georgian is a faint echo of the Arabic, which connects this persecution with the ritual suicide cult said to have been practised in India by certain fanatical devotees: 'And then self-incineration and the burning of corpses became a custom in the land of the Indians, because of the bliss which the adherents of this creed claimed to be attained through such incineration. And volunteers from among them started burning themselves voluntarily, in order, so they asserted, to attain the same merit as those martyrs.'

(Jerusalem Georgian, fols. 12r.-17v.; Bombay Arabic, 32-6; Greek Barlaam, pp. 35-49, but omitting all reference to cremation or voluntary self-immolation.)

V

When Iodasaph grows up, he suffers from the loneliness of his condition. One of his guardians explains the reason for his seclusion. Eventually, the prince prevails on his father to let him out. When he goes riding, he catches sight of a blind man, a cripple and an old man. Learning that everyone is subject to infirmity and death, his zest for life abandons him.

(Jerusalem Georgian, fols. 17v.-24v.; Bombay Arabic, pp. 36-41; Greek Barlaam, pp. 49-61.)

VI

The holy hermit Balahvar (Barlaam) appears from the land of Sarnadib (i.e. Serendīb, Ceylon), disguised as a merchant. He gains access to Iodasaph under the pretence of having a precious jewel to show the prince. When asked about the nature of the jewel, he tells the parables of:—

1. The Trumpet of Death
2. The Four Caskets
3. The Sower.

(Jerusalem Georgian, fols. 25r.-34r.; Bombay Arabic, pp. 41-5; Greek Barlaam, pp. 62-77. Note that the hermit's name is changed by the Greek to Barlaam, no doubt through confusion with the fourth century Antioch Saint Barlaam or Barlāhā, in praise of whom a discourse was composed by St. John Chrysostom. In the Greek, Barlaam comes from Senaar or Shinar, that is Mesopotamia: cf. Genesis, xi. 2. Note also that in the Greek, the parable of the sower is woven into Barlaam's introductory homily.)

VII

Balahvar continues his conversation with Iodasaph and demonstrates through parables the vanity of earthly things:—

4. The Man in the Chasm and the Elephant
5. The Three Friends
6. The King for One Year
7. Dogs and Carrion
8. Physician and Patient
9. The Sun of Wisdom

(Jerusalem Georgian, fols. 34r.-47r.; Bombay Arabic, pp. 46-60; Greek Barlaam pp. 78-133, 146-227, but omitting Parables 7 and 8, and substituting a unicorn for the elephant in No. 4.)

VIII

Iodasaph enquires why his father is oblivious of the true faith. Balahvar replies with further parables:—

10. The King, the Believing Vazir and the Happy Poor Couple
11. The Rich Youth and the Beggar's Daughter
12. The Fowler and the Nightingale

(Jerusalem Georgian, fols. 47v.-72r.; Bombay Arabic, pp. 60-88; Greek Barlaam, pp. 133-45, 227-53, 273-301.)

IX

The prince's tutor, Zadan, is suspicious at Balahvar's frequent visits. Iodasaph invites Zadan to listen in to one of their conversations. Zadan expresses sympathy with Balahvar's ideas, but is concerned at the king's anticipated reaction to these developments.

(Jerusalem Georgian, fols. 72r.-75r.; Bombay Arabic, pp. 88-91; Greek Barlaam, pp. 300-9. Tutor's name not given in Arabic; becomes Zardan in Greek.)

X

Balahvar tells Iodasaph that he must return to his companions in the wilderness. The prince wants to accompany him, but Balahvar dissuades him by a parable:—

13. The Tame Gazelle

Balahvar and Iodasaph exchange clothes, Iodasaph receiving the ascetic's tattered hair apron. Balahvar relates:—

14. The Costume of Enemies

(Jerusalem Georgian, fols. 75v.-86r.; Bombay Arabic, pp. 91-9; Greek Barlaam, pp. 252-73, 309-17.)

XI

The king learns from Zadan that Iodasaph has become a Christian. Dismayed at the news, he consults the soothsayer Rak'is (Rakhis). The latter advises Abenes to try to capture Balahvar; as an alternative he recommends summoning his former master Nak'or (Nakhor) who strongly resembles Balahvar and could be made to impersonate him and allow himself to be overcome in a mock debate on the faith.

(Jerusalem Georgian, fols. 86v.-90r.; Bombay Arabic, pp. 99-101; Greek Barlaam, pp. 318-27. The character of Nakhor is introduced for the first time by the Georgian redactor; in the Arabic, there is only one soothsayer, Rākis.)

XII

Rakhis pursues Balahvar, but only succeeds in capturing some monks, whom the king chops to pieces. Nakhor appears on the scene, to impersonate Balahvar. Learning of the stratagem planned by the king together with Rakhis and Nakhor, Iodasaph threatens Nakhor with dire consequences if he fails to make the Christian faith prevail in the forthcoming debate. Nakhor triumphs on behalf of the Christians and is himself converted.

(Jerusalem Georgian, fols. 90v.-115v.; Bombay Arabic, pp. 102-62, with numerous other episodes added; Greek Barlaam, pp. 327-439, where the Greek redactor inserts into the story for the first time the *Apology of Aristides*, which Nakhor recites, thereby convincing the assembly and winning the day.)

XIII

King Abenes then consults the magician T'edma (Thedma), to whom he tells a story:—

15. The Amorous Wife.

Thedma recommends that Iodasaph be exposed to the wiles of women in order to cure him of his religious zeal, and tells a story:—

16. The Youth who had never seen a Woman.

Iodasaph resists the temptation, Thedma being confounded.

(Jerusalem Georgian, fols. 116r.-124v.; Bombay Arabic, pp. 163-70, where Budhasaf is made to beget a son; Greek Barlaam, pp. 440-505, but omitting story of Amorous Wife, doubtless as unseemly.)

XIV

King Abenes resolves to divide up his realm between himself and Iodasaph. The young prince's domains prosper, while his father's decline. The king is convinced of the truth of Christianity, and is converted together with all his followers, including Thedma. After the death of Abenes, Iodasaph hands the whole kingdom over to another Christian, Barakhia, and departs to Sarnadib. There he is reunited with Balahvar, and they both die in the odour of sanctity.

(Jerusalem Georgian, fols. 124v.-172r.; Bombay Arabic, pp. 170-83, where Budhasaf's act of renunciation, departure for his spiritual mission, various travels and adventures and final death are told in a way far closer to the Buddhist traditions; Greek Barlaam, pp. 505-611. Note that the name of Barakhia (Barachias) as Iodasaph's successor, and the episode of Iodasaph's reunion with Balahvar are introduced for the first time by the Georgian redactor, and then taken over and elaborated in the Greek; in general, the conclusion of the Christian adaptation has been radically altered to fit in with the ideals of early Christian asceticism.)

CHAPTER V

ST. EUTHYMIUS THE GEORGIAN AND THE GREEK BARLAAM ROMANCE

As suggested in the last chapter, the newly discovered Jerusalem Georgian text, *The Life of the Blessed Iodasaph*, represents the first specifically Christian treatment of the story of Budhasaf, or the Bodhisattva. Its dependence on the Arabic non-Christian book of Balauhar and Budhasaf is emphasized by the discovery in this Georgian version of three parables from the Arabic, 'Dogs and Carrion', 'Physician and Patient' and 'The Amorous Wife', which are found neither in the Greek nor in Christian redactions in any other language. It was further pointed out that the names of several actors in the story—Balahvar, Iodasaph, Rakhis—are taken directly from the Arabic, as is the name of Balahvar's retreat, Sarnadīb, for Serendīb.

This investigation may now be taken a stage further, in order to show when and how there came into being the perfected Greco-Byzantine romance of Barlaam and Ioasaph from which derive so many versions in diverse tongues. Recourse will be had to evidence both internal and external, that is, to comparison of the texts and to clues left by writers of the period under review.

It is noteworthy, to begin with, that the Greek Barlaam romance reproduces in Hellenized form those proper names which the Georgian had already inherited from the Arabic. Balahvar becomes Barlaam, no doubt after the St. Barlaam of Antioch who was martyred under Diocletian and later praised by St. John Chrysostom in one of his discourses; Iodasaph becomes Ioasaph, a name which Woodward and Mattingly have explained as meaning 'The Lord gathers'; Rakhis becomes Araches. The Greek version also takes over and suitably modifies names which have no close equivalent in the Arabic, but are first found in the Christian Georgian. Thus, King Abenes becomes Abenner, after Abner, who features in the Old Testament as Saul's general; Barakhia, a Biblical name first introduced in the Georgian, is retained in the form Barachias; the sorcerers Nakhor and Thedma reappear as Nachor and Theudas, the latter being the name of a magician mentioned in the Book of Acts as well as by the historian Josephus; the tutor Zadan becomes in Greek Zardan.

In the few pages left, it is hardly feasible to embark on a thorough-going textual comparison of the Greek and Georgian versions, though a few pointers have been given in a study contributed to the volume of essays dedicated to Sir R. L. Turner.[1] It is to be hoped that means will before long be found to edit and translate the new and more complete Georgian text from codex No. 140 of the Jerusalem collection.

Meanwhile, it is important to note the far greater sophistication with which the Greek redactor has treated Barlaam's exposition of Christian doctrine, compared with the plain and unvarnished sermons Balahvar preaches in the Georgian prototype. The writer or writers who completed the Greco-Byzantine version obviously enjoyed showing his or their conversancy with the Holy Scriptures and early Church Fathers. In addition to scores of quotations from the Bible, there are frequent reminiscences of such respected authorities as St. Basil, St. Gregory of Nazianzus, St. Athanasius of Alexandria, St. Cyril of Jerusalem, St. John Chrysostom, St. John Climacus, St. Maximus Confessor, Nemesius of Emesa and St. John Damascene.

In fact, the abundant quotations from the last-named writer have led some scholars to revive the attribution contained in certain later mediaeval manuscripts, and to sponsor the view that the Greek Barlaam romance was entirely composed by St. John of Damascus in person. But one swallow does not make a summer, and the fact that a work contains quotations from a certain author is no proof that it was entirely written by that author. In reviewing a recent monograph on this theme, Professor Glanville Downey rightly says that 'the use of parallel passages to prove identity of authorship is notoriously a delicate undertaking, fraught with danger.' With particular reference to comparisons cited in support of St. John Damascene's authorship of the Greek Barlaam, Downey considers that 'one must apparently add a further note of query about the value of such parallels,' especially as some of the supposed references to works of St. John Damascene turn out on examination to be simply quotations from the Bible or from well-known liturgical texts.[2] In short, one cannot help agreeing with Father

---

[1] To be published as Vol. XX of *Bulletin of the School of Oriental and African Studies, University of London.*
[2] *Speculum*, XXXI, 1956, pp. 166-8.

François Halkin when he asks: 'Can one not conceive that a Greek man of letters, a monk of Athos or Constantinople for example, might be permeated by the writings of St. John Damascene to such an extent as to know them virtually by heart, and borrow quotations and reminiscences from them on every possible occasion?'[1]

One addition made by the final redactor of the Greek Barlaam and Ioasaph romance deserves special mention. This is the early Christian text known as *The Apology of Aristides*, which has been inserted virtually entire into the story under guise of being the magician Nachor's speech at a public debate where Nachor is impersonating the hermit Barlaam (Balahvar). This *Apology of Aristides* is a very cogent piece of polemic against the religions of the Ancient Greeks, the Chaldaeans, the Jews and the Egyptians; it is supposed to have been presented to the Emperor Hadrian, or possibly Antoninus Pius, by an Athenian philosopher called Marcianus Aristides. The original Greek of the Apology was thought to have been lost by the time of St. Jerome, though it was preserved in the Sinai Syriac text as well as in Armenian and Greek fragments which came to light at various times. It then turned out that the *Apology of Aristides* had all the time been preserved virtually complete in the Barlaam and Ioasaph romance, masquerading as an oration by an Indian sorcerer![2]

In the Georgian versions, that is to say, in both the Jerusalem *Life of the Blessed Iodasaph* and the abridged *Wisdom of Balahvar*, there is no trace of this Apology at the appropriate point in the narrative, but merely the remark that Nakhor's speech was more eloquent than anything that Balahvar himself could have produced. The Georgian texts do not give a single word of the actual discourse in support of this assertion. It is clear that whoever put the Barlaam and Ioasaph story into Greek had at his disposal a manuscript of the *Apology of Aristides;* coming to this point in the work, he took his cue from the Georgian version's bare reference to Nachor's excellent harangue and put into the latter's mouth this effective piece of Christian apologetic. Thereby he enhanced the effect of the episode, and gave concrete evidence for Nachor's astounding success against the idol-worshippers.

In looking for the author or adapter of the Greek Barlaam and

---

[1] *Analecta Bollandiana*, LXXI, 1953, p. 478.

[2] J. Rendel Harris and J. Armitage Robinson, *The Apology of Aristides*, Cambridge 1891 (Texts and Studies, Vol. I, No. 1) ; R. L. Wolff, 'The Apology of Aristides—A Re-examination', in *Harvard Theological Review*, XXX, 1937, pp. 233-47.

Ioasaph romance, one should accordingly seek for an individual or group familiar with the Bible, the lives of the saints and the works of the early Church Fathers; who lived later than St. John of Damascus (c. 676-749), whose writings are quoted extensively in the Greek version; and who possessed fluency in both Georgian and Greek.

In mediaeval Byzantium, there were several cosmopolitan monastic centres where these conditions could have been satisfied. One of the foremost was Mount Athos, where from the tenth century the Great Lavra of St. Athanasius was a foyer of Greek culture under the patronage of the Byzantine emperors, and with ready access to the great libraries of Constantinople. In close proximity was the Athonite Iviron or Georgian monastery, founded about 980 as an offshoot of the Great Lavra, and also enjoying Imperial favour and protection. In spite of national rivalries and antagonisms, the cultural life and even the administration of the Greek and Georgian monastic communities were closely intertwined.

In connecting the final evolution of the Greek Barlaam romance with Mount Athos, one is not confined to mere speculation. With minor divergences, no less than four separate sources, in three different languages, agree in testifying to the Greek Barlaam's Athonite provenance, and they all name the same person as translator.

To begin with, a fifteenth century copy of the Greek Barlaam and Ioasaph romance preserved in Paris, Gr. 1771, states in its heading that Euthymius the Georgian, *kathegetes* or administrator of the Great Lavra of St. Athanasius on Mount Athos, had rendered the story from Ethiopic (!) into Greek. The eleventh century Venice manuscript of the same work, Marc. Gr. VII. 26, describes the tale rather confusingly as having been brought back from Ethiopia to Jerusalem by the monk John of the Monastery of St. Saba, and then translated from the Iberian or Georgian tongue into Greek by or on behalf of Euthymius the Georgian, a worthy and virtuous man.[1]

Nor is this all. The manuscript of the earliest Latin translation of the Greek version, preserved in the National Library at Naples, No. VIII, B.10, has a heading describing the work as 'The Story of Barlaam and Iosaphat, brought to Jerusalem from inmost

[1] D. M. Lang, 'St. Euthymius the Georgian and the Barlaam and Ioasaph Romance', in *B.S.O.A.S.*, XVII, Pt. 2, 1955, p. 307.

Ethiopia by John, a venerable monk of the monastery of St. Saba, and translated into Greek by the holy man Eufinius (sic)'. In the preface to this Latin rendering, the anonymous translator writes:

'In the sixth year of Constantine Monomachus, Augustus, the most holy, the lord triumphator (i.e. A.D. 1048-9), I was ensnared within the curving walls of the mistress of cities by Imperial duties; and my eager desire for intensive research led my intention among Greek books, that I might set down something worthy of remembrance, taking it, like a bee, from the various flowers of the Achivi. This I was driven to do by the continual contemplation of my solitude, so far from home, pondering the present, and fearing the future. With my troubles as incentive, while my mind was fluttering hither and thither, a certain man named Leo handed me a book.

He begged me, for the sake of an offering to God, and for the memory of the Holy Barlaam, that I translate from the Greek into Latin, in simple language, this unknown work from the Ancients, never before translated, and up to my time completely buried in oblivion. Then anxiety for work and brotherly love urged me on, so that eagerness for activity spurred me to undertake a task of whose performance literary inertia was disapproving. And strengthened by the prayers of my brother, I bound myself to translate word for word and sense for sense, after the manner of the Ancients, and also undertook to make the sense clearer in the proper places, or in part to change it, so that my editing would at once render it delightful reading for the diligent, and stop for ever the mouth of the carpingly critical.'

Just before the end of his translation, the anonymous Latin writer adds a passage further explaining the circumstances in which he undertook the work. He says here that the first person to translate the story from the 'Indian' idiom into Greek was a monk called Eufimius, by nationality an Abasgian or Western Georgian. Following in the footsteps of this Eufimius, the translator had undertaken to render the book into Latin through the encouragement of a certain noble man called Leo, son of John; this was in the year 1048 after Christ, when the writer was in his sixtieth year and the thirty-first of his residence in Constantinople.[1] These indications, of course, tally well with the clues given

[1] R. L. Wolff, 'Barlaam and Ioasaph', in *Harvard Theological Review*, XXXII, 1939, pp. 133-7.

by the two Greek manuscripts; they are important as showing that the Greek Barlaam was a complete novelty to residents in Constantinople about the year 1048, who regarded it as a recent importation from oriental literature, and not as a work of an established Church Father like St. John of Damascus.

Further information is provided by Georgian sources of the period under review. In the biography of St. Euthymius the Athonite (*c.* 955-1028) composed not long after his death by his successor, St. George the Hagiorite (1009-65), it is stated that Euthymius translated 'Balahvari', that is to say, the story of Balahvar and Iodasaph, from Georgian into Greek.[1] It is also clear from other indications that George the Hagiorite regarded Iodasaph as first and foremost a saint of the Georgian rather than of the Greek Orthodox Church: in the Georgian Church calendar which George the Hagiorite drew up according to the Byzantine model, he entered the saint's name in the Arabo-Georgian form 'Iodasaph', and not as 'Ioasaph' as in Greek; what is more, he put him under the date of May 19, which is quite at variance with subsequent Greek usage, where Ioasaph features on August 26.

Now George the Hagiorite, though a Georgian patriot, was a meticulously orthodox Byzantine churchman, intent on remodelling the Georgian ecclesiastical order on Greco-Byzantine lines. If, as some scholars assert, the Greek Barlaam and Ioasaph romance had been written three centuries earlier by St. John of Damascus, and Ioasaph had already been enshrined among the saints of the Greek Church, then George the Hagiorite could not possibly have entered the saint in his Church calendar in a form of name and under a day quite at variance with subsequent Greek usage. Furthermore, St. George the Hagiorite composed a hymn in honour of St. Iodasaph, based not on any Greek source, but on material deriving from the Georgian *Life of the Blessed Iodasaph*. The Georgian scholar Pavle Ingoroqva has established that George the Hagiorite's date for St. Iodasaph was taken over from the so-called Klarjo-Meskhian or Georgian national synaxary, completed by about A.D. 900.[2]

All this is corroborated by the fact that none of the Greco-Byzantine calendars of Saints in which St. Ioasaph features are even as early as the time of Saints Euthymius the Athonite and

---

[1] Lang, *Lives and Legends of the Georgian Saints*, p. 155.
[2] See Shalva Nutsubidze, *K proiskhozhdeniyu grecheskogo romana Varlaam i Ioasaf*, Tiflis 1956, pp. 230-3.

George the Hagiorite, let alone John of Damascus, a fact which was specially emphasized by Peeters and Father Halkin. This, of course, is yet another reason for rejecting the supposed connection of St. John of Damascus with the Barlaam romance: had Saints Barlaam and Ioasaph been vouched for by so eminent an authority as the great Damascene, why should the Greek Church have waited three centuries before recognizing their existence? If the complete Greek text of the Barlaam romance had been in circulation since before St. John's death in A.D. 749, it is also an odd coincidence that none of the scores of Greek manuscripts is earlier than the time of St. Euthymius the Georgian; the earliest dated copies recorded are apparently Escurial No. 163 of A.D. 1057 and Magdalen College, Oxford, Greek No. 4 of A.D. 1064. The conclusion is inescapable that all the talk in the prologue to the Greek Barlaam about holy men bringing the work direct from India direct to Jerusalem for St. John Damascene to turn into Greek is a pure fraud, designed merely to gain the exotic story a wide circle of enthusiastic readers.

The real translator, St. Euthymius the Athonite, is a well-known historical figure whose biography has been handed down in Georgian as well as in Greek versions (Nos. 4467 and 4573 of the Lampros catalogue of Greek manuscripts on Mount Athos). The father of Euthymius, John Varazvache, was a nobleman at the court of David Kuropalates, prince of Tao in Georgia. Tiring of ceremonial life, he became a monk and went to live on Mount Olympus in Greece, leaving his young son, Euthymius (born about 955), with relatives in Georgia. These relatives later handed the child over to the Greeks to be held as a hostage for the fidelity of the Georgians to the Byzantine emperors. Euthymius lived for some years in Constantinople, becoming deeply imbued with Greek culture.

When news of this reached John on Mount Olympus, he emerged from his retreat and proceeded to the Imperial court. Finding Euthymius speaking and writing Greek fluently, John made arrangements for his education to be completed and then took him back to Olympus. Euthymius was entrusted with revising and completing the Georgian version of the New Testament, and with translating into Georgian many works of the Greek Fathers. After John and Euthymius and their kinsman, the soldier-monk John Tornik, had founded the Iviron Monastery on Mount Athos, Euthymius ultimately became its abbot, as well as holding an official position in the Great Lavra of St. Athanasius. He was offered the archbishopric of Cyprus, which he refused. In 1028, Euthymius was killed at Constantinople in a street accident while on a visit to the Imperial court; his memory was cherished not only by the Georgian monks on Athos but by the Greeks also, a special memorial service or *acolouthia* being held annually in his memory (Greek text listed in Lampros, Athos catalogue, No. 4650).

On the basis of the Athos, Jerusalem, Tiflis and other manuscript collections, Professor Kornili Kekelidze has enumerated over 160 titles of biblical and patristic works rendered from Greek into Georgian by St. Euthymius. Many of his translations have been preserved to this day, including a few in the saint's own autograph. As his biographer, George the Hagiorite, puts it, 'the blessed Euthymius went on translating without respite and gave himself no repose; day and night he distilled the sweet honey of the books of God, with which he adorned our language and our Church. He translated so many divine works that nobody could enumerate them, since he worked at his translations not only on Mount Olympus and Mount Athos (which works we can list in detail), but also in Constantinople, and while travelling, and in all kinds of other places.'[1]

Euthymius also composed one or two original works, including a set of directives addressed to Theodore the Priest of St. Saba concerning liturgical practice and approved and forbidden Church books;[2] a manual of ascetic rules, composed for a disciple under the title, 'Regulations for the Mode of Life befitting an Ascetic or Hermit' (according to Kekelidze, this manual was first composed in Greek and then translated into Georgian); also attributed to Euthymius is the freely rewritten Georgian version of the original Greek biography of St. Hilarion the Iberian, who died at Thessalonika in 875.[3]

In spite of his sixty years in Byzantium, doubts have been expressed in some quarters whether Euthymius, as a Georgian, could have possessed a sufficient mastery of the Greek idiom and Greek patristic literature to enable him to re-fashion the Barlaam romance in its present elaborate guise. But that is not quite the

---

[1] Lang, *Lives and Legends of the Georgian Saints*, pp. 161-2, where some of the translations are listed.
[2] Georgian text published by M. Sabinin in *Sak'art'velos samot'khe* ('The Paradise of Georgia'), St. Petersburg, 1882.
[3] K. S. Kekelidze, *Dzveli k'art'uli mdserlobis istoria* ('History of ancient Georgian literature'), 3rd. edition, Tiflis, 1951, pp. 182-4.

point. Since Greek and Georgian monks lived side by side on Mount Athos, competing with one another in religious and literary works, it would have been more than sufficient if Euthymius had simply furnished a literal Greek rendering of the Georgian *Life of the Blessed Iodasaph* as a rough draft for his Greek colleagues to embellish at their leisure. From 'Ioasaph' in Greek to 'Josaphat' in Latin is but a painless transition; and so the Bodhisattva enters Western Europe as a saint of the Christian Church.

Thus it was that after capturing the imagination of the Manichaeans of Central Asia, the Arabs of Baghdad and the Georgian Christians of the Caucasus, the Bodhisattva attained a fresh incarnation as a holy man of European Christendom. Even though the Middle Ages lacked direct knowledge of the Buddha's teachings, yet his legendary life story contributed to the spiritual formation of the age. That Gautama Buddha was venerated for centuries as a Christian saint, far from providing a theme for sarcasm or scandal, should be regarded as proof of the universal appeal and the spiritual virility of the teachings of Śākyamuni.

PEDIGREE OF BARLAAM AND JOSAPHAT

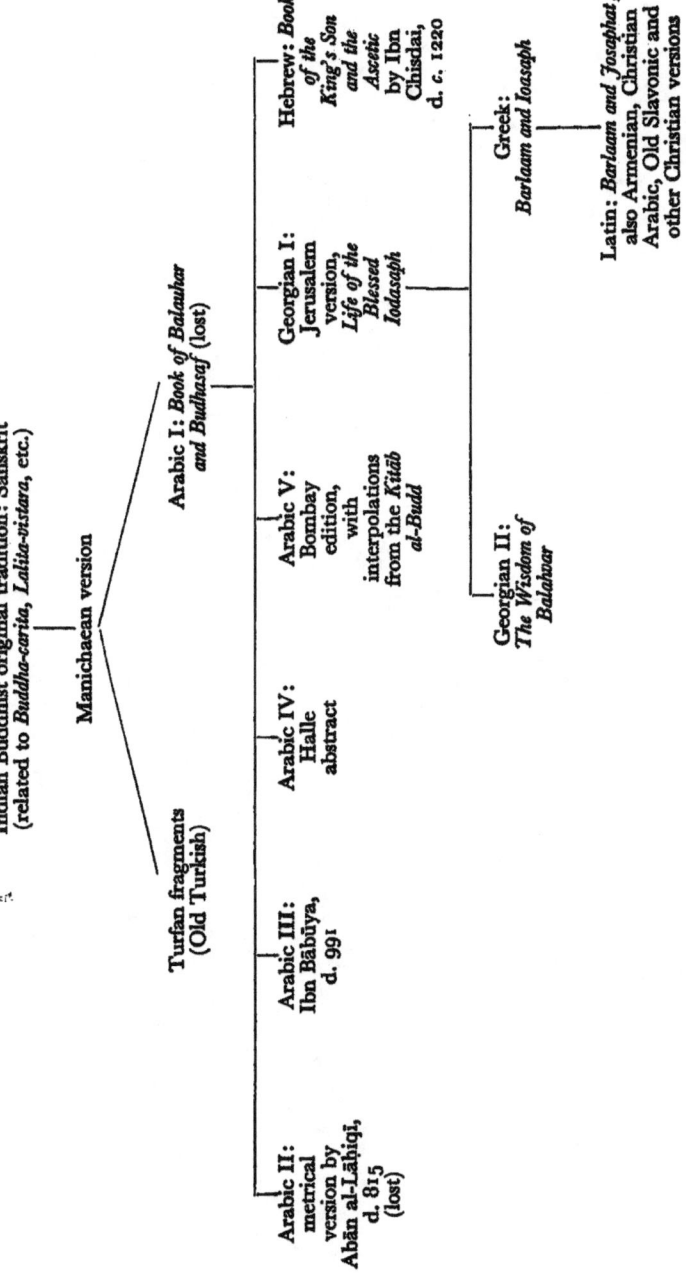

PART TWO

THE WISDOM OF BALAHVAR

A CHRISTIAN LEGEND OF THE BUDDHA

Translated from the Old Georgian Version

THE WISDOM OF BALAHVAR

May 19: Commemoration of Iodasaph, King of the Indians *

This story was told to us by Father Isaac, son of Sophronius of Palestine. It is the book which is called *The Wisdom of Balahvar*, the man who dwelt in the wilderness among the hermits.—Grant us thy blessing, O father!

Once I travelled to Joppa and found this book there in the library of the Indians. In it are recorded such deeds of this world as serve to edify the soul exceedingly.

There was a certain king in the land of India, in the place which is called Bolayt, and his name was Abenes. He was a pagan, an idolater, but a man of peace-loving and humble character, and extremely charitable to the poor. He had no son and was sorrowful because of his childlessness, for he was enormously rich and longed for an heir to whom he might bequeath his treasures. He prayed therefore to those gods of his, that they would grant him issue. But they were impotent to perform any good thing for his sake, and so his prayers to them were all in vain.

Nevertheless, God, who desires the life of all mankind, as a recompense for the charity which he bestowed upon the poor, granted him a fine and comely child. So he was filled with great joy. And he named him Iodasaph, and said: 'This is what my gods have done for me!' And he glorified these all the more, and gathered together a crowd of astrologers and philosophers and soothsayers, so that they might tell him what lay in store for his son.

Then they all declared with one voice: 'This child shall attain a reign of glory such as nobody has ever achieved in the land of India.'

But there was among them one man more steeped in wisdom than all the others; and he said to the king: 'This I judge, O king: The glory which this child shall attain is not of this world; but I believe that he is to be a great guide upon the road of truth.'

---

* This heading added in Jerusalem manuscript No. 36; the date is that laid down for the commemoration of St. Iodasaph in the Georgian menaia or calendar of Church ritual drawn up by St. George the Hagiorite (1009-65).

When the king heard these words, he was filled with sorrow and forthwith ordered the servants of Christ to be expelled from his land. And he sent a crier to proclaim: 'Thus speaks King Abenes. —If after three days any of you Christians are still to be found, I shall destroy you all in the direst torments.'

One day, however, as the king was going out to survey the country outside the city, he saw two men, servants of God, coming away from the town. So he said to them: 'How comes it that you have made so bold as not to leave my country? Or did you fail to hear what my crier proclaimed?'

They answered him: 'Behold, we are just about to leave.'

Then he said to them: 'What was it that delayed you until now?'

They said: 'The lack of provisions for the journey.'

The king said to them: 'Those who stand in fear of death do not dally for the sake of provisions.'

And they said: 'Had we been afraid, we should indeed have made haste to go; as it is, we expect to find rest in death.'

The king said: 'And how can you speak thus, now that you are leaving my kingdom through fear of me? How can you say you are not doing this from fear of death?'

And they said: 'It is not through fear of death that we are making our departure from your country, but in order to avoid furthering your evil deeds or providing you with any pretext for godless conduct.'

Then he let them go, but issued orders that however many Christians they detected, they were to burn them all with fire.

Now King Abenes had in his service a certain man whose name was Balahvar. And he was a servant of God and a believer, and he obeyed Christ's commandments. The king loved him greatly, for he was intelligent and prudent and a fine scribe, and he was the most favoured of all in the king's sight. King Abenes was unaware that he was a slave of Christ, and bestowed greater honour upon him than on any of his other dignitaries.

On one occasion this man Balahvar was going along the road when he saw a man lying, wounded by a wild beast; he had lost the limbs of his feet and of his hand; and the man was weeping. And Balahvar asked him: 'O man, why is it that you are in this state, and you weep?'

The man told him: 'I am a patcher of words, and I have been

mauled by a wild beast and deprived of my limbs. Now if anyone succours me, I will be useful to him in the day of need.'

Balahvar paid no attention to these words of his, but none the less had pity on him; and he ordered his slaves to lift the man on to a horse and bring him back home to his house. And he told his chamberlain to look after him well and provide for his needs.

But the idolaters became hostile to Balahvar, because they envied the honour accorded him by the king. So they told the king: 'O king, that man in whom you have placed your trust does not belong to your faith, for if he meets any of those Christian fellows, he greets them with cordiality. And now he desires your downfall and is plotting to seize your kingdom. Whenever he encounters any who are exiles from your realm, he immediately makes friends with them and favours them.'

The king said to them: 'If it is not as you allege, then evil is in store for you.'

Thereupon the king summoned the man of God and began to test him, saying: 'You know how much absorbed my mind has been in this world; now that my days are drawing to a close, I see that I have been toiling in vain, and I am afraid that my end may overtake me, and that I may be found wanting. So I wish from henceforth to be united with the servants of God and work to attain the life eternal. Now what say you, O faithful one and counsellor of mine?'

When the man of God heard this, his spirit was moved and he wept. And he said to him: 'O king, live for ever, since instead of what is transitory, you have chosen what is eternal and far better; because the glory of this world is as nothing—like a shadow it passes by and like smoke it vanishes. Now carry into execution this intent of yours, for it is good that by renouncing this transitory world you should win in return the world everlasting.'

These words made a painful impression on the king, who was filled with resentment on account of this man; but he did not reveal it to him.

Then Balahvar realised that a snare had been laid for him, but he did not know whence the snare came. He became very despondent, and passed that night without sleep. Then he remembered that man who was a patcher of words, and he called him and said to him: 'You told me that you can cure a person who has been wounded by words'.

The man said to him: 'It is indeed so, but heaven forbid that you should now be in such a way afflicted.'

But he said: 'All this time I have been serving the king, and never once have I seen him angry towards me, for I have walked before him in faithfulness. But today I have seen him incensed against me, and I think that there is no peace in his heart.'

The man who was maimed asked: 'What dealings have there been between you and him?'

But he said to him: 'All I know is that he made a certain pronouncement to me, and I summoned him to better things. I believe that he was tempting me.' And he related everything to him.

Then the maimed man said to him: 'I will cure these words by the grace of Christ and the power of the Cross. Know this, that the king is malevolently disposed towards you, for he suspects you and believes that you intend to seize his realm. Arise then tomorrow, and shave off the hair of your head and remove those garments of yours, and put on a hair shirt, and thus enter in before the king. If he asks you what this signifies, tell him: It concerns the matter for which you summoned me. Behold, I have made myself ready, because I have no desire for life without you. After I have shared in the good things of your reign, it is my duty at this time to share with you also the hardships of this world. Like those ones who have already been tormented by you, let me also be tormented in your company, so as to win eternal virtue together with you.'

So that man did as the maimed one had taught him. And the malice departed from the king's heart, and he was wrathful at Balahvar's denouncers. But Balahvar was very joyful, and let the hair grow once more upon his head.

Then the princes were again filled with envy because of Balahvar, and they said to the king: 'O king, if you examine Balahvar's throat, you will observe there a cross which he adores; and he makes a mockery of our gods.'

The king, however, thought that they were telling lies about this man. And he touched him with his hand, and saw the golden cross upon his breast, and said to him: 'What is this delusion of yours, O Balahvar?'

But Balahvar said: 'O king, I am not deluded, for ever since my childhood I have been serving Christ and worshipping the Cross on which He outstretched His arms for our salvation—but this without being in any way remiss in your service. And now, since the name of God, Christ, has been revealed upon me, I will no longer deny His Godhead, even though you tear apart my flesh or burn it with fire; but I shall confide my soul into His hands.'

The king said to him: 'Do not speak so, my beloved Balahvar, for you are a man noble and distinguished in my eyes. And if you will worship my gods, I will grant you other cities also, and I will empty out my treasure houses upon you, for you are greatly beloved in my sight. But if you will not do this, I will wear out your flesh with savage tortures and remember no longer my love for you.'

Then the man of God took off his golden belt, adorned with precious stones, and laid it before the king and said: 'If the crown of your kingdom were set upon my head, not even for the sake of this honour could I deny my belief in Christ. And if you wear out my flesh with tortures, you will not succeed in shaking me either, for the good things of heaven, in which we rejoice eternally, are loftier than those of earth: and the torments of hell are more bitter, wherein those who oppose and deny God are doomed to suffer. But I, O king, am ready for the torture. Do not delay, so that I may depart before my time and come before my King to rest there for evermore.'

At these words, however, the king was softened and said to him: 'Woe is me, my beloved Balahvar! How could you destroy my hope and disobey my command? Depart now from my land, and let no report of you reach my ear. But if ever I encounter you again, I will give no warrant whatsoever for your blood.'

Then this man of God abandoned transitory glory, and went away to join the hermits and serve Jesus Christ, our God.

Then the king built a city for his son, and ordained that his child should reside there. And he commanded that no old man should be allowed to live therein. He provided trusty slaves to serve his son, and gave him Zandan as his tutor. And he admonished the latter, and told him that no old man, nor any sick person, should on any account be shown to the boy, nor should death ever be mentioned to him; for he wished him to be brought up in joy and happiness, without encountering any form of affliction in the shape of either old age or infirmity or death.

And as the child grew up in the splendour of youth and perfection of body, his father took prompt measures to ensure that he should lack none of that instruction in knowledge which is fitting for a king. And the child was most receptive of knowledge, a cherisher of learning and a seeker out of all words of wisdom. The king for his part was filled with amazement at the boy's prowess; and owing to the words which the astrologer had uttered, he would allow nobody to enter in and visit him. But he himself used to come frequently, for he loved him.

Now since the king admitted no one to him, nor would let him leave the city, he began to repine and to brood over this order of things, and finally said: 'My father is in authority over me, and knows what is best for me.' But when he had attained the wisdom of perfection, he said in his heart: 'I am grown up. Why should not I choose what is best for myself? Why should not I find out what is the cause of this detention of mine?'

Then he said: 'If I ask my father regarding my detention, he will not tell me the truth, and I fear that I might plunge him into agitation.' So he began to behave with enhanced respect towards his tutor. And he treated him with great honour and promised him yet more for the future, and said: 'If you tell me the truth concerning the thing which I am going to ask you, you shall find still greater distinction in my sight when I become king. But if you do not tell me the truth, you will put an end to my love for you.'

Zandan answered and said: 'I will tell you the truth, O king's son; only keep secret everything I relate to you.'

When he had confirmed this, he said to him: 'What is it that you desire?'

Then Iodasaph the king's son said: 'What is this confinement of mine within this city?'

The tutor answered him and said: 'I will expound the matter to you and give you the precise explanation.—When you were born, your father made great rejoicing, and summoned all the astrologers and consulted them regarding your birth. Then they all predicted for you the attainment of great renown. However, the wisest one of all said: This son of yours will achieve great glory of majesty; and I believe that he is to be a great guide along the path of truth, and he will become an opponent of your faith and will preach not those gods to which you accord service and subjection.—For this reason, your father was afraid lest you might disobey his will and adopt an alien creed and entertain affection for those men, the servants of God.'

And the lad said: 'And what kind of men are the servants of God?'

Then he replied: 'They are the same sort of men as we are; and they serve God in heaven. But your father tortured some of them, and others he burnt with fire, and others he expelled from his dominions.'

And Iodasaph, the king's son, said to him: 'And are none of them to be found in our country any more?'

But he said: 'No.' And when he had explained everything to him, he made no further answer.

When his father came, he said to him: 'I should like knowledge of a certain matter, which has plunged me into a state of great sorrow and despondency.'

Then his father said to him: 'Ask, my son!'

He answered him: 'Tell me, my father and lord, what was the reason for imprisoning me in this place, and why do you prevent people from visiting me?'

He said to him: 'It was in order that nothing should afflict your heart, my son, and so that I might avert all ills from you.'

The lad said to him: 'Know, O king, that by the conduct you have adopted towards me you have turned all my joys into bitterness, for my soul longs to go outside the gates. So now I beg you to release me and let me survey the land; and never will I transgress your command.'

When he heard this, the king's heart sank, and he said within himself: 'If I stand in the way of his will, his sorrowfulness will increase and I shall be sacrificing all his joy.' And he said: 'My son, if you so desire, mount your steed today and go out among men and let it be according to your will.' And the king commanded those who accompanied the lad to send out heralds in front: if they found any old man, or any affected by illness, they should remove them apart out of the highway, so that he might not look upon the condition of mankind, nor be in any way grieved by their transitory lot. And they did so.

One day, however, as the lad was going along, he caught sight of two men, one of them deformed and one a blind man who was bearing the other along; and he became fearful and made enquiry concerning them. And they said to him: 'These are men, and they are stricken with infirmity, just as other men also are stricken.'

And he said to them: 'Does this happen to all men?'

But they said: 'No, but to certain ones; for to some people this occurs, while others escape it.' Thereupon he was disturbed in his mind, and turned away in downcast mood.

And again he was going out on one occasion; and his retainers who preceded him were negligent, and failed to notice an old man lying helpless, whose hair was white as wool; and not a tooth was in his mouth, and his speech was mumbling. And as the king's son went by, he saw him and was horrified, and said to Zandan his tutor: 'What is that?'

But he said: 'That also is a man.'
And Iodasaph said to him: 'What has brought him to this state?'
But he answered: 'The length of years.'
And he said: 'What is a year?'
Zandan answered: 'Twelve months.'
And he said: 'What is a month?'
He answered: 'Four weeks.'
— 'And at what term of years does one become like that?'
He answered: 'At eighty years, or maybe a hundred.'

But he was broad in intelligence and filled with wisdom, and he reckoned up the months and the years and said: 'As I observe, day follows swiftly upon day, and year upon year; and the end of a hundred years soon comes to pass. What awaits that man now?'

Zandan said to him: 'Hereafter, death.'
And Iodasaph said: 'What is death?'
But he could conceal nothing from him any more, and said: 'The memory of that man vanishes from the earth.'
And Iodasaph said: 'Will my father become like this as well?'
And he said: 'Yes, he will become so.'
— 'And you too, just the same?'
And he said: 'Yes.'
He said: 'And I likewise?'
— 'You likewise as well.'
— 'And all men in the same fashion?'
— 'Yes, in the same fashion, if they reach this life span. But know this also, that certain of them are only just born when death carries them off straightway; and others, when they have grown up but a little; and others yet, when they have just reached manhood.'

And he said: 'So death is due to come upon me then?'
And he said: 'Not upon you alone, but upon all mankind.'

Then the king's son was dismayed, and his heart welled up; and he wept, and spoke to Zandan his tutor, saying: 'Does no country exist where mankind is not overtaken by such affliction, like those infirm beings I saw previously, and this man I see now? This time, death seems to me harsher still!' And once more he beat his breast and wept and said: 'Tell me whether there is a country in which I may escape from afflictions?'

Then Zandan the tutor wept also and said: 'There is no such country under the heavens, O king's son, in which men may escape from afflictions and from death.'

And again he asked: 'And what will men become after death?'

The tutor said to him: 'Those men who were servants of God used to speak thus: God is in heaven above, and He gave birth to the skies and to the earth, to the seas and the deeps, to the sun and moon and stars, and by His command are brought into being the tempests of the winds, the thunder and the gales, so they said; and He created man from the earth by His hand, and He breathes into him His immortal spirit. And if anyone serves Him and walks within His commandments and worships Him, they say that heaven and paradise are in store for him, and after death, he will be carried thither, and therein he shall rest. But of your father's philosophers, some say that the soul is mortal, and others, immortal.'

When Zandan had uttered all these words, the king's son turned away and went off to his own apartment; and he said within his heart: 'No longer do I find any pleasure in this transitory life, now that I have seen and listened to all these things.' And from then onwards he pondered what he should do, and esteemed no more the delights of this world. However, in spite of all this, he was fond of his father, and when he used to visit him he would start to regain his spirits. But when he left, he would say in his heart: 'O God of heaven, send me a man from among Thy servants, that he may teach me the way of truth, and that I may walk within it and perform Thy holy commandments.'

At that time, Balahvar learnt from the Holy Spirit that the king's son longed to look upon the men who served God. He arose and departed from the scene of his ascetic life, and came out into the world. And he put on merchant's clothing and took with him a small box. And he came to the gate of the king's son and said to the gatekeeper: 'Go in, and tell Zandan that a stranger who has arrived from a far-off land is calling for him.'

So the man went in; and when he had given the message, Zandan the tutor came out.

And Balahvar said to him: 'I have a precious gem, and if you will, pray accept it for the king's son; because it is finer than red brimstone, since it gives sight to blind men's eyes and hearing to the deaf, and makes the dumb speak, and cures the infirm, and enriches the needy and makes men victorious over their foes, and fulfils all the heart's desires.'

The tutor said to him: 'My good man, you do not look a fool to me, although your words are presumptuous and I fear lest you might cause me to deceive the king's son. Show it me now, so that I may examine it and inform him about it accordingly.'

Balahvar said to him: 'No one has the power to see it unless he possesses two qualities: soundness of eyesight and purity of body. But if someone of defective vision and steeped in sin should catch sight of it, the light of his eyes would be extinguished as well as the intelligence of his mind. Now I am a physician, and I perceive the defects of your vision and fear lest the light of your eyes be quenched. But I have heard about the pure life of the king's son; and he is a lad, and sharp of eye, and he has the power to see it. Now have no qualms about informing him, for if you produce this thing to him, great honour will be vouchsafed to you, more than that of your fellows.' And he showed him the box which he had with him.

Then the tutor went in to display this before the king's son, and told him everything he had heard from Balahvar. Now the boy's spirit longed for the society of men, so that it might hear from someone words profitable to the soul. And when the tutor related to him the strange story concerning this gem, he sensed in his spirit that he had found his desire; and he commanded the man to be brought in before him.

When he had made his appearance before the king's son and greeted him, then the king's son, as is fitting, courteously asked after his health, and told the tutor to leave him. And he commanded Balahvar to show him that gem.

Balahvar answered him and said: 'It would be unfortunate if any untoward event befell you: for my treasure has the properties your tutor described to you. If anyone feeble of wit should see it, he is deprived of his eyesight. But now I desire to test you by speech, and then, if it be possible, I will display it to you, for I have brought it for you and for no one else. And I place my hope in God, that you have attained the ability to look upon it; and also that you may come, if God will, to cherish me, O king's son, wretch that I am, and pay me honours beyond compare.'

The king's son answered him: 'This will I perform, in return for the edifying discourse I am to hear from you.'

FABLE THE FIRST

The Trumpet of Death: The Four Caskets

Then Balahvar said: 'Even if you do vouchsafe this to me, it is nothing to be amazed at; for once upon a time there was a king who was virtuous and sought after righteousness. And when he was passing along the road one day with a throng of followers, he caught sight of certain men clothed in ragged and torn garments, with complexions of yellow hue. But the king recognized them, and he quickly got down from his horse and embraced their necks. And when his noblemen saw this, they considered it extravagant conduct, but did not dare to interfere. Then they went to see his brother, who used to speak his mind frankly to him; and they said to him: "Tell your brother never to do such a thing again, for he has made obeisance to ragged men." So he came and told the king about this affair; but he gave him no answer.

'And it was the custom in that kingdom that when the king was angry with anyone, he sent his slaves and the trumpet of death was sounded before the man's gates. And after a few days he sent slaves and told them: "Go and blow the trumpet of death at my brother's gates." So they went and did so.

'When the king's brother heard this sound, he was afraid and began to weep and repine. Afterwards he put on mourning garments and went out with his wife and children to the gates of the king his brother; and they sprinkled ashes upon their heads. Then he ordered them to be led into his presence. But they wept. And the king said to him: "How is it that you were afraid at your brother's herald? Do you not know that your brother and the heralds are mortal men and unable either to hasten the fulfilment of His will, or to avert what is destined to come upon them? And how was it that you were astonished at my falling down before those who were the heralds of Our Lord Jesus Christ, who were reminding and warning me of eternal condemnation? Thereby I have been made aware of my many sins against Him. But I shall unmask the conduct of those people who complained to you about me, saying: "Why ever did he make obeisance to the servants of God?"

'Then on one occasion he entered his treasury and fetched caskets adorned with gold and jewels. And he also had a load of stinking refuse brought, and dead men's bones and other loathsome trash. And he stuffed all this inside the caskets and fastened them on top with his seal. Then again he fetched other caskets, of plain manufacture, smeared with tar; and he placed within these some precious gems and whatever he could find that was best in his treasury, in addition to many perfumes. And these he sealed up also. Then he summoned his noblemen together, and when there was merrymaking, he ordered his treasurer to bring the caskets. And when he had laid them out, he told his nobles to appraise the caskets. But they failed to fathom the matter, and said to the king: "One of these lots of caskets is unworthy to be brought inside your palace, but the second group of them is valuable beyond price."

'Then he ordered those caskets whose value they estimated highly to be opened. They threw them open, and there arose a nauseous stink, from which they all shielded their faces with their sleeves. And they tipped out all manner of loathsome stuff. But then he ordered the mean-looking caskets to be opened; and there arose from them the scent of perfume which concealed all the disgusting smell. And out of these they tipped adornments of great price and precious jewels.

'And the king said: "Understand this, all you noblemen: it is we who are these caskets made beautiful without, we who deck out our exterior with multi-coloured apparel, whereas our soul within is full of sin and filth. But those who humble themselves for the sake of God and His name, and embrace poverty with fasting and prayer, and become yellow of complexion—the soul of these within is full of fragrance like the perfume stored within those caskets; and they shine before God just as do those precious gems. Now do you blame me for greeting those men of God, whose inward being is like to this?"

'And this is a semblance of you, O king's son, for you have granted me honour in return for the trust which you have conceived towards me.'

Then Iodasaph arose from his throne and said: 'Blessed am I, for I have found what my soul longed for and I have been seeking.' And he turned and said to Balahvar: 'Good are your words and true; and I imagine them to be that jewel which you keep hidden. For they strengthen my heart and lighten my eyes and fortify my understanding; and if the matter be as I believe, then bestow your words on me instead of the jewel, and remove the sorrow from my heart.'

FABLE THE SECOND

The Sower

Balahvar said to him: 'The mouth of God speaks to the people in the parables of the Gospel.—A sower went forth and began to sow. And some fell on the roadway, and the birds pecked it up; and some upon the rock, on which there was no soil, and it sprouted up and withered, because it had no roots attached; and other seed—among thorns, and it sprouted up and the thorns choked it; but some fell upon good ground and sprouted up and brought forth much fruit.

'Now that sower is the Giver of wisdom, and the seeds are the words of truth. And the ones which fell on the roadway and were pecked up by the birds are those which are heard by the ear, but pass the heart by; and the ones which fell on the rock and sprouted up and withered are those which are listened to for a moment and then make no firm impression on a person's mind, and wither away; but the ones which the thorns choked are those words which a man cherishes, but when they sprout up within him, he chokes them by ambition and the distractions of worldly affairs. But those which sprouted up and brought forth much fruit are the ones which the eye harvests, and the heart gathers in and the mind brings to perfection; and so it overthrows ambitions and cleanses the heart from sins and brings forth fruit.'

The king's son said to him: 'I place my hope in God, that whatever seed you implant in me may sprout up well and bring forth fruit. Now describe to me the likeness of the transitory world, and how it deludes men.'

FABLE THE THIRD

The Man and the Elephant

Balahvar said: 'This transitory life resembles a man pursued by a raging elephant. And it cornered him inside a fearsome abyss.

Then he caught sight of some trees on to which he climbed, and then saw two mice, one black and one white, which were gnawing away at the roots of the trees up which the man had clambered. And he looked down into the chasm and noticed a dragon, which had parted its jaws and was intent on swallowing him. And he looked up above and saw a little honey trickling down the trees, and he began to lick it up. And now he remembered no longer the peril into which he had fallen. But the mice gnawed through the trees, and the man fell down, and the elephant seized him and hurled him over to the dragon.

'Now, O king's son, that elephant is the image of death, which pursues the sons of men; and the trees are this transitory existence; and the mice are days and nights; and the honey is the sweetness of the passing world; and the savour of the passing world diverts mankind. So the days and nights are accomplished and death seizes him and the dragon swallows him down into hell: and this is the life of men.'

And the king's son said: 'You have revived my spirit by this parable. Now convey to me the aspect of this world and of those who love it.'

FABLE THE FOURTH

The Man and his Three Friends

Balahvar said: 'The aspect of this world is like this:— A certain man had three friends. One of these he loved more than the others, and the second one he also loved; but the third friend was without consideration in his sight. Some time later, the king's minions apprehended that man and were going to haul him off for trial. And he went to his favourite friend and said to him: "You know, my beloved friend, how dear you are to me. Now behold, they are hauling me off for trial. Help me in my trouble." He answered him and said: "I am no friend to you now, and I do not even know you; I have other friends with whom I can make merry. But I will give you two garments, though these will not fit you." And he went to his second friend and said to him: "Remember now that love which I had towards you. Behold, I am being hauled off for trial, so help me in my trouble." He answered: "I have no time to bother with you today, for I have enough trouble of my own. Go your way: from now on I am no longer your friend. However, I will accompany you a little way and then return to look after my own affairs." Then he went to his third friend, whom he detested, and said to him: "I am overcome with shame, but I am in trouble and so have come to you. Help me, although I have not behaved well towards you." But he said to him joyfully: "I am your friend, and I have stored up the memory of your little kindnesses. And now I will repay you with interest and accompany you and intercede for you in your trouble, and not deliver you into the hands of your enemies." Then that man began to repent and said: "Why did I not bestow upon you all the favours I vainly wasted on those two friends?"

The king's son said: 'Explain to me the significance of this also, O holy one!'

Balahvar said to him: 'That first friend is the love of money, which people are greatly fond of; and they cannot take it with them when death carries them off and presents them before the judgement seat. But the two garments are shrouds. And the second friend is wife and children, who are dearly loved by a man, and he takes thought for them constantly; and on the day of judgement they can avail him nothing, but follow only as far as the tomb and then turn back to look after their own cares. And the third friend is his own soul: and he does no good thing for its sake. But what little he does is held of great value in the sight of God, and God repays it a hundredfold.'

The king's son said to him: 'I realise that you are making the whole truth known to me. Now tell me a parable to show how illusory is this world, and by what means it is possible to win deliverance from it.'

DOI: 10.4324/9781003250760-11

FABLE THE FIFTH

The King for One Year

Balahvar said: 'I will tell you by what means.—Now there exists a certain city, and the custom there is that they make a foreigner king for one year. When the year is over, they strip off the royal purple from him and with just two garments they drive him off into exile. On one occasion, however, they elected a certain man; and getting to know of the bad custom of that city, he sought out strangers and poor men and secretly handed them objects of value for them to take to that country whither they were going to banish him. And when they sent that man into exile and he arrived at the place, he found everything he had sent on well treasured up, and received sevenfold benefit from it; and now he is making merry for all time.'

The king's son said to him: 'Expound this also to me.'

Then he said to him: 'In truth, this city is the whole world, and men govern and reign over it. And they know that in time to come they must die and be committed to burial wrapped in two shrouds; and all the life of men is one day, and death and committal to the tomb is banishment. But he who is prudent with wisdom gives secretly to the poor, to strangers, to the weak, the hungry and the naked, and he will be charitable, peace-loving and humble in heart. But God, who sees the things which are hidden, rewards their charity publicly with good things stored up where the thief cannot steal nor the moth corrupt; and therein a man shall rejoice for ever and ever.'

Iodasaph said: 'Have such words as these never been made known to my father? For by the discourse which you are pronouncing to me my heart is lit up and my mind made glad, and my spirit rejoices greatly.'

Balahvar said: 'They have never been accurately made known to him.'

And Iodasaph said: 'And why have the wise men taken no action to effect this?'

Balahvar answered: 'Because they were aware of his unreceptive frame of mind. And therefore they have delayed communicating this, since they could find no occasion of gaining a hearing from him.'

Iodasaph said: 'What a pity that this should be so, just because they could not find an opportunity to relate this to him!'

DOI: 10.4324/9781003250760-12

FABLE THE SIXTH

The King and the Happy Poor Couple

Balahvar said: 'Here is a parable concerning the kingship of one who governed the affairs of this transitory world; and he had a counsellor, a righteous and pious man who eschewed all evil-doing and encouraged the king in every deed beneficent to men, for he was a religious and god-fearing person. And when he saw the king bowing down before idols, he was very perturbed and grieved, like someone who laments for a son. And often he desired to discuss religion with him, and he consulted his friends about this question. But they said: "You are familiar with his inner habit of thought and if you find an opportunity, then speak to him; but it is as well to be circumspect, for the devil is unsleeping in the cause of evil, and it would be a bad thing if he incited him against you and disaster befell you."

'And this man sorrowed greatly for the king's sake. And the king said to the man one night: "Come, let us go for a walk in the town tonight, so that we may see the doings of the people." They went out, and in the course of their walk, they came upon some large garbage heaps. And the king looked and saw some light, as of a fire, issuing forth. And when they drew near, they saw what looked like a cave hollowed out of some of the refuse. Inside were a man and a woman dressed in clothes made of old rags; and as they gazed, the sound of singing was heard coming forth. And the man was at table, seated on a pile of manure, while the woman danced in front of him and flattered him with praises such as befit kings. And she called him Lord, and he addressed her as Queen, and both of them were gay and merry.

'But the monarch and his counsellor looked on for a long time and attentively observed their behaviour, and went away amazed. And the king said to his companion: "Never have we enjoyed our life like those poor folk do, nor are we as happy as they; and I suppose that all their days are passed in this fashion."

'The counsellor now found his chance to speak, and said: "Do not imagine, O king, that the glory and dominion in which we revel are valued to the same extent by those who live through God's service. The gold-sculpted mansions which we build for ourselves, and the beauty of paintings and the splendour of raiment—these they admire not at all; for they see the temples of heaven, not made by hand, and raiment invisible to the eye; and they rejoice because they enjoy felicity for ever and ever in the things which God has prepared for those that love Him."

'And the king said: "Are the sages aware of this condition of things?"

'But he said: "There are indeed men who serve God and have abandoned all the things of this world and are in love with eternity, because they have tried out this world and found it all profitless and impermanent."

'The king said: "And what is the eternal kingdom? Is it not liable to sadness?"

'The counsellor said to him: "The eternal kingdom is infinite bliss, not subject to sorrow; and prosperity, not subject to poverty; and joy, not subject to affliction; and health, not subject to sickness; and royalty, not subject to extinction; and tranquillity, not subject to fear; and life uninterrupted by death, for it is eternity imperishable. And all this falls to the lot of those that love Him."

'The king said: "Can there be any man worthy of this place, or able to enter into it?"

'The counsellor said: "The gate is barred against no one who is willing."

'The king said: "What is the road thither? Tell me!"

'He said: "The service of the one God who made all things that are created."

'The king said: "And what has hindered you up to now from telling me about this road?"

'The counsellor said: "The terror of your majesty."

'The king said: "If the matter stands thus, we ought not to remain idle. Now we must toil in order to attain there the life of untroubled peace."

'And the counsellor said: "Is it now your command that I should apprise and remind you regularly about this from time to time?"

'He said to him: "Not from time to time; but let your vigilance be active incessantly day and night."

'And afterwards the king began to serve God and became worthy to enter that place of which his counsellor had told him; and they both won life eternal.'

Iodasaph said to Balahvar: 'No longer does any love whatsoever for this world exist in my mind, but I long for the life eternal; and now it is my intention to remain with you and endure the austerity of your way of life.'

DOI: 10.4324/9781003250760-13

FABLE THE SEVENTH

The Rich Youth and the Poor Maiden

Balahvar said: 'If you do this, you will be like that rich man who received a poor girl as his daughter-in-law. For we have heard that once there lived a certain youth, the son of a rich man. And his father had sought out a maiden, the child of noble parents, to be a bride for his son. But he did not consent to this, and ran away from his father. And in the course of his journey he caught sight of a daughter of poor parents, dressed in humble garments, sitting on the threshhold of her dwelling while she busied herself with her handwork and rendered thanks to God.

'The youth said to her: "Who are you, O maiden, and for what blessings are you thanking God?"

'But she said: "O man of scant knowledge, do you not know that a little medicine saves a person from great illnesses, and likewise a little thanksgiving wins greater blessings? But I am the daughter of a poor old man, and I am waiting for the grace of God."

'Then the youth called to the old man. He came out and the youth said to him: "If you are willing, give me your daughter to be my wife."

'He said to him: "The daughter of poor folk is not fit to be your wife, for you are the son of rich parents."

'The young man said to him: "It is because I have perceived the wisdom and intelligence of your daughter that I aspire to take her as my wife. And behold, the daughter of rich parents was betrothed to me, and I refused to take her as my bride. And if you will perform this, you will find me a man of virtue, if the Lord so will it."

'The old man said to him: "Though you aspire to take my daughter as your bride, your father will not consent."

'But he said: "If he will not consent, I will settle here."

'Then the youth went into the old man's house, took off his apparel, and put on poor man's raiment. And the old man began to test him and weigh up his understanding. And when he found him to be intelligent, and discovered that his love did not derive from passion alone, he took him by the hand and led him into his treasure house, and showed him precious objects of such beauty that he had never seen any to compare with them. And he said:

"Son, all this is yours. Enjoy it from henceforth." And the youth was filled with joy.'

Iodasaph said to him: 'Let this parable be applied to me, if the Lord wills it. But you tell me that the old man tested him. How then do you propose to test me?'

He said: 'Fear God, and follow His command, and shun the behests of the world. And God will not bring your works to ruin, and will not test you beyond your strength. And I for my part will beseech my Lord Jesus Christ, who created heaven and earth, and pray to the Holy Trinity which has no end, terrible and gracious, powerful and merciful, invisible and inexpressible, regal and benevolent towards men, omniscient and not oblivious, before which tremble all that are created, that He will cleanse you, to be a true mentor of righteousness and an exemplary model of piety, a giver of sight to the blind, of hearing to the deaf, a lover of the saints and detester of sins, until He causes you to attain in our company those abodes which He has promised us through the mouth of the holy prophets and apostles in whom we set our hope, that we may become worthy to join their company.'

At these words Iodasaph's heart welled up within him, and he began to weep and said again to Balahvar: 'Of what span of years are you?'

But he said: 'Twelve years.'

And he said: 'How can you tell me this, for you are a venerable man of sixty years and more.'

Balahvar replied: 'Counting from the time I was born, I am sixty years of age, but it is only twelve years since I dedicated myself completely to God. Previously I was dead, but for the last twelve years I have been alive.'

Iodasaph said: 'How is a man dead, who eats and drinks? And if you do not deem that first life to be any life, neither can you attach any importance to temporal death either.'

Balahvar said: 'Is not my readiness for self-sacrifice plain to you from my coming to see you? For you know the evil disposition of your father towards me. The reason is that I am not afraid of death, so long as I die in God's service.' Then he related to him all his life in detail, and for what reason he had gone away into the wilderness.

Iodasaph said to Balahvar: 'Describe to me the likeness of wisdom, and why this nation of ours has a fondness for idols.'

FABLE THE EIGHTH

The Fowler and the Nightingale

He answered: 'A certain man caught a nightingale and was about to kill it. But she said to him: "Why do you wish to kill me? For you cannot satisfy your appetite on me. If you will release me, I will teach you three precepts. And if you will observe them, you shall benefit thereby."

'So he agreed and let her go. And she perched on the branches of some trees and said: "Do not strive after the unattainable; do not regret what is past; whatever thing you would not like, do not do to anyone else; and you shall live."

'But wishing to test that man, to see whether he would observe these precepts, she said to him from up aloft: "My good man, if only you had acted wisely and killed me! In my crop there is a pearl as big as an ostrich egg. If you had extracted this, it would have brought you a great price."

'When the man heard this, he began to feel regret, and wanted to catch her again and kill her. And the man said to her: "Regarding the precepts you have taught me, I have no other way of repaying you but this.—Enter now into my house, for the winter season is harsh, and I will look after you well. And I will provide you with good entertainment, and let you go."

'The nightingale said to him: "My teaching of maxims to you is all in vain, for you have broken all three precepts at this very moment: because my setting at liberty is already done and past, and now you are regretting it; to catch me is something unattainable, and you are striving after it; and you do not desire your own death, but you long to murder me. However, I was just testing you to see whether you are observing the precepts. How could you believe that in my crop there is a pearl as big as an ostrich egg? For even with all my feathers on, I am not even a fraction of the size of an ostrich egg!"

'Therefore, O king's son, whatever instruction you may give to stupid people, they are still not convinced; and they reject the commandments of God and affirm things which they have thought up in their own heads, for they have manufactured idols with their own hand and they worship them as gods and say: "These are our saviours from evil." And they squander their wealth on these; for devils abide within them, and they believe in them. And they do not realise that God is one, the Father and Ruler of all, the Maker of heaven and earth; also Our Lord Jesus Christ, and the Holy Spirit, which proceeds from the Father. He alone is the Creator of all, and all others are created; He alone is timeless, and all others are temporal; He alone is strong, and all others are weak; He alone is high, and all others are low. And everything was brought into being by Him, and apart from Him not one thing was made. And He is gracious, merciful, patient and full of compassion and love towards men, and He has prepared abodes of joy for those that obey Him, and abodes of torment for the disobedient. It is He, mighty in three persons and one essence, who has made you a seeker of His will, in order that you might live through the power of the Trinity which is of a single essence. But if you observe His commands, then you will realise how excellent are His teachings.'

Iodasaph said: 'What is it that God wills?'

He answered: 'It is God's commandment that whatever you would desire for yourself, you should do to your neighbour; and whatever you would not desire, you should not do to another; abide in prayer and supplication day and night, and you shall have His Cross for the vanquishing of your foes; for it is thereby that He has saved me from the pains of death.'

Iodasaph said to Balahvar: 'By observing the commandments, shall a man fulfil God's will?'

Balahvar said: 'Yes, he shall fulfil it indeed.'

—'Seeing that there are such excellent things in the world, why then have you rejected them?'

Balahvar said: 'Two things impel us to do this.—First, the fact that the supreme blessings of God cannot be compared with the trifling joys of the realms here below. And whoever shall strive, he shall receive the greater honour. A friend may well come to feel no small jealousy towards his fellow; after all, people who pay merely what tax is due are not on the same footing as those who give free bounty.

'The second is this: Beware of indulging in proffered delights, whereby one is involved in unseemly doings and incurs condemnation. But if you shun them, you will receive peace and comfort abounding. If someone leads his flocks to the pasture, he is not in his right senses if he dozes off or becomes careless, so that the flocks are completely scattered; rather is it when he has driven them home from the pasture that he can sleep and rest with a quiet mind.'

Iodasaph said: 'You are telling me the entire truth. Add however a further discourse to make me grow in hate and detestation of this world.'

Balahvar said: 'Let this be quite clear to you, that revulsion from the world conciliates God. Since this life is short, and the days and nights soon flow away, let us now make an effort to abandon the world voluntarily, for willy-nilly, we are fated to leave it. Even if our life be long drawn out, death is yet in store for us. Then all a man's possessions shall be scattered abroad and his lofty buildings ruined; and his name shall become unknown and his memory wiped out; and his body shall shrink away; for they shall carry him forth naked from his dwelling-place and consign him to the dark cavern and lay him down by himself in a strange place, forsaken in his wretched state by those that hate him. And everyone shall revile him, even his wife, brethren and children.'

At this, Iodasaph wept and said: 'Your words have pierced my heart. Speak now to me concerning the life.'

And Balahvar said: 'I, O king's son, was greatly fond of this world and absorbed in its delights. And when I had taken thought and seen the vicissitudes of those who dwell in it, I realised that no one can endure therein, neither great nor small, neither strong nor weak, neither wise man nor fool. Then I perceived that I too must pass away as they passed away, and am subject to change just as they have changed, since I am no greater than the great nor stronger than the strong; and whatever has befallen them must befall me also, for all of us shall expire and be dissolved. And when I had realised all this, I sought out for myself some better way, and although it appeared to me a hard thing, I held myself in contempt and renounced my ambitions and bridled my own will, that it might not lead me astray and plunge me into the distractions of this world.

'And I heard the word of God out of divinely inspired books, saying: "I have created this world and all its semblance as something transitory. Take up now provisions for the way, for you shall depart into a strange land. Be vigilant, because it is certain that you shall pass over to the other side: and I have prepared an eternal mansion in which are two habitations; one is the abode of all good things and a place of unspeakable delight for those who have loved me and observed my commandments, and therein they enjoy everlasting bliss; but the second abode is full of torments, privation, shame and dishonour and arrogant wrath, so that retribution may be meted out to those that hate me."

'When I heard this voice, I realised that its words are just, and I took up provisions for the way, so that I might attain to the abode of peace. And I flee from that fearsome abode and am greatly afraid, for many are my sins; howbeit, greater still are the mercies of our God.'

Iodasaph said: 'How is it possible to enter into that good abode?'

Balahvar said: 'Through quitting the world and all its preoccupations. For it behoves a wise man to train himself like a wise shepherd trains his flock; and the fear of God is fully and ever present in his mind. For the Psalmist says: "The fear of God is the beginning of wisdom: a good understanding have all they that do His commandments." Know this too, that no man can absorb all wise teachings. Which of men can partake simultaneously of all the kinds of food and drink which he may see and his heart take a fancy to? Rather should he partake of them little by little, according to his capacity.

'But be mindful of this also, that the devil tempts the mind, saying: "Unless you abandon God, you will have to fast forty days, and go about in mourning, ashes and tears." Such hardships as these he invokes, with a view to distressing people and thereby causing them to waver. Alternatively, he is liable to puff them up with pride exceedingly, and then cast them down to earth and deliver them to great affliction.

'Thus it behoves you to discipline yourself and fear God. Observe this, and learn it well, and arm yourself with the Cross; and may the God of peace be with you in all your doings. For there exists no power and resource whereby to withstand the resources of the enemy, except it be vouchsafed to us by Our Lord Jesus Christ.'

Iodasaph said: 'Expound to me the glory of God.'

Balahvar said: 'Inexpressible is the likeness of the Godhead, and the mind cannot succeed in fathoming it. Neither are any tongues capable of worthily praising Him, because the knowledge of Him is inaccessible to created beings, apart from what He has revealed by the mouth of the prophets. He appeared to the world, He who from the beginning was with the Father, namely Our Lord Jesus Christ. His words are true, that His likeness is invisible to the eyes; and the apostles and prophets testified concerning Him. And men believed as a result of His signs and miracles: for the dead were raised, the blind received sight, the lame were made to walk, the devils were cast out, and all diseases cured by power such as was given to no one else. And everything which He desires is done in the heavens and on earth, in the seas and in all the depths.'[1]

Iodasaph said: 'What is the evidence for the knowledge of God?'

Balahvar answered: 'The heavens and the earth and all that dwell therein, things spiritual and creatures endowed with flesh. If you see some implement which has been fashioned, even though you may not have seen its maker, you believe all the same that it had someone to make it. Similarly, in the case of a building, even if you cannot see the man who built it, your reason still tells you that it has a builder. As for me, when I looked at myself and examined my anatomy, I realised that I had a Creator. When He so willed, He gave me birth and shaped me quite apart from my own choice. If I had been my own creator, I should have made myself greater in beauty and in perfection of body. But He who gave me birth made me inferior in some ways and superior in others. And I realised also that He will bear me away out of this life without asking my consent. When I had taken thought, I became conscious of the workings of our life, namely that we are unable either to add to, or take away from our stature: neither can we renew what has grown old, nor fasten on afresh any limb which may have fallen away. No king can perform this by his sovereignty, no clever man by his cleverness, no wise man by his wisdom, no strong man by his strength.

'Then again, we observe the drawing in of evening following the day, and the revolutions of the spheres: and thereby we know that all things have a Creator. And He is not of the same nature as the things which He has created; if He did resemble them, He would be affected by the same forces which govern the things which He has created. Whatever He says, will be, and whenever He so wills, it will forthwith pass away; and again, He can restore it to being, just as it was at first. For His command is sharper than a double edged sword and swifter than a lightning flash. And if He so wills, he can annihilate everything and then revive it. And blessed and glorious is His name for ever more.'

Iodasaph said: 'All this you have truthfully testified. Yet how do

[1] This passage occurs in Jerusalem manuscript No. 36 only.

you know whether there is to be any resurrection after death, and any repayment for good works and evil?'

Balahvar answered: 'There are two things which make this manifest.—For there is a discrepancy between the way of life of the devout and that of the unbelievers in this world, and we see many unbelievers ending their life in contentment, but observe the devout leaving this world in straitened and despised circumstances. Thereby one knows that God, the just judge, has forborne from glorifying His devout ones simply in order to bestow upon them even greater honour at the resurrection; but the unbelievers He shall judge according to their works.

'In the second place, this is made evident through the preaching of the apostles, who were personal witnesses of the glory of God. It is to this end that they uttered glad tidings of eternal reward for the faithful, and gave warning of everlasting torments. And we cherish their testimony because they displayed signs and miracles among men by the power of the only-begotten Son of God, which is Our Lord Jesus Christ.'

Iodasaph said: 'Since the apostles were men of ordinary human stuff, what leads you to believe that they were telling the truth?'

Balahvar said: 'We know the truth thereof, as I told you previously, from the fact that they followed Our Lord Jesus Christ and renounced their possessions, and embraced a life of poverty; and because they enriched the poor by their word and themselves went about bare-foot and bare-headed with but a single garment; and they mortified themselves and instructed others in similar wise. Now if they had been false prophets and liars, they would not have led men along such narrow and difficult paths. They would have been more likely to set before them those objects which delight men, and to have shown them a broad and spacious gate, calculated to please the eyes and captivate the heart. And they would have pandered to their lusts and enjoyments and won over the hearts of men by this kind of conduct, and not put fear into men's hearts by prayer and fasting, austerity and poverty.'

Iodasaph said: 'If any man were to arise and falsely declare himself an apostle of God, how can it be detected whether he is telling the truth? Or is this impossible to detect?'

Balahvar said: 'His works will declare his hidden secrets. For such people preach long-suffering and are themselves incapable of patience; they teach virtue, and are themselves full of vice; nor are they capable of performing any miracle which surpasses the powers of man.'

And when Balahvar was instructing the king's son by such teachings as these, and Balahvar's visits to Iodasaph were multiplied, Zandan the tutor said to him: 'You know, O king's son, that your father set me over you because of my fidelity. Now I am amazed at the conduct of this man, who is coming to see you all the time, and I fear that he may belong to the number of those who are hostile to your father. Now if you please, desist from this affair and from talking with him. Or if you prefer, let me clear myself from blame by reporting the matter to your father. If you will not consent to this, then dismiss me and let your father give you other servants instead of me; and so relieve me from your father's wrath.'

Iodasaph said: 'First do this: stand apart, hidden behind the curtain, and listen for a little while to what he says to me. Then do whatever you think fit.'

And when Balahvar came in before Iodasaph, Zandan was standing by himself behind a curtain.

At the outset of their conversation, Iodasaph made enquiry concerning the passing world. But Balahvar started to declare the vanity of the passing world and said: 'It behoves those who seek after transitory things to choose in preference that bliss which is eternal and imperishable. Why is it that people are unaware of the swiftly fading nature of this world's glory? For they see the rapid dispersal of riches; and those who amass them expend their efforts in vain, since after a little while others will be the proprietors of their treasures. What worldly deed is deserving of praise, or what treasures remain free from decay? Rather will those for whom riches are piled up here below encounter woe and poverty there above; and those who reap honour here will find disgrace there above.' And much more after this style he taught him.

When Balahvar had left, Iodasaph wanted to test Zandan, to see whether he had been edified by Balahvar's words. And he said to him: 'Do you not hear what this liar and charlatan is telling me? For he is trying to pervert me and spoil the enjoyment of this life.'

Zandan said to him: 'You have no need to resort to ruse with me, O king's son. For this discourse is luminous, and we have heard and recognized its great sweetness. Since the king persecuted the worshippers of God and expelled them from this country, from thence forward we have heard such doctrine no more. And we know that we have turned our back on it through folly and we have given our affection to this temporal world which quickly passes away. But if, O king's son, you find this doctrine pleasing and have chosen it for yourself, then you must be prepared to endure and take upon your head the burden of it, as well as the king's wrath and the opposition of the nation.—Be joyful then in the glory of heaven and in the life eternal! I, however, am unshaken in my love for the world and my awe before your father, though I do not deny the merits of this cause. Pray advise me how I may escape from your father's wrath, for I have so far concealed this affair from the king.'

Iodasaph said: 'If you will hide this matter from the king, I assure you that this in itself is loyalty towards him, to spare him from being plunged into grief and worry, and deprived of hope in his posterity, thereby falling into depression. From now onwards, be not afraid of me—do and say whatever you think fit, for I have become conscious of the vanity of this world and realise that man is nothing but worm and putrefaction, dust and ashes, swiftly to be scattered. Therefore I take no thought for the body, for it has no existence; but the spirit exists, sensitive to pain or every joy. For this reason, one should take heed lest it be delivered over to eternal and unending torment, to fire and the unsleeping worm, and to outer darkness. Know this as well, that I have found for myself a Father, the Ruler of all, the Creator of the heaven and the earth, and the Maker of all creatures that are born; and I fear Him and tremble before Him and bow down to Him, for He is the King of kings, and He has power over souls and bodies, and His is the dominion for ever and ever.'

But now Balahvar wanted to depart, and he took leave of the king's son. Iodasaph was very sad and could not bear to be separated from him, and said: 'I cannot endure to exist without you, and I beseech you to let me go away with you, and let us dwell together in the company of your associates.'

FABLE THE NINTH

The Tame Gazelle

Balahvar answered: 'O king's son, this situation recalls to mind the story of a certain nobleman, who had a beloved son. And for his son he reared a wild gazelle, and attached a little bell to its neck. It used to go out to graze in the fields according to its wont, but on one occasion it joined with other gazelles and followed them off into the forest. When they discovered that the gazelle had gone off into the depths of the woods, its keepers went off to search for the gazelle and found it in company with other wild animals. These they slew, and they seized the gazelle and took it home.

'You would bring a like fate on the heads of me and my companions. Your aspiration would not be fulfilled, nor would you be able to bear the hardships which I and my associates endure. Know also that it is better for you to abide in this place; and if it please God, you shall succeed through other means in making yourself pleasing to Our Lord Jesus Christ.'

Iodasaph said: 'Tell me, what is the form of nourishment whereby you subsist in the wilderness?'

He answered: 'We feed ourselves on the herbs of the earth. But when we suffer any lack, we receive food from the believers, our brethren.'

Iodasaph said: 'I beg you, take as much treasure as you desire, to satisfy the needs of yourself and your companions.'

He answered: 'How can you give any treasure to my companions, since the least of them is richer than you?'

Iodasaph said: 'How comes it that the poorest of your companions is richer than I? For you talk a great deal about their poverty.'

Balahvar answered: 'I say so because those of you who have, are anxious for more; and they are very much concerned not to lose anything, and bustle up hill and down dale in their efforts to amass more. But my companions take no care for anything, neither for food nor for clothing, since these they derive from the grass according to their needs, and they glorify God thereat: as they have quitted the world's wealth and mundane vanities, they are happy and rejoice in spirit as they wait for the kingdom of heaven. But those who seek after riches here below, however wealthy they be, are yet poor in mind and cannot be satisfied. My associates, however, dwell in great tranquillity here below, for their treasures are stored up in heaven where no thief steals nor moth corrupts. And in these you too shall have a share, to enjoy bliss for all eternity.'

Iodasaph said: 'Whereby do we know the truth of this matter?'

And he said: 'We know its truth through the fact that when any of my companions departs from the body, then we see angels of light coming to bear away his soul in accordance with the Lord's command; and we hear sweet singing which proceeds from the mouths of the angels. And as they carry away his spirit, then the veil is removed from our eyes and we see that soul borne aloft in the angels' hands, ascending up to heaven. And we direct our eyes upon them until they vanish into the shades which stand guard over the heavens.

'As for the treasure which you have in mind to give to my companions, give it all to the poor and needy. I am not sent by my companions in order that I should make available to them a poison which troubles the mind of men. How should I set before them that very foe which they have put to death and trampled under foot? Those who are rich indeed, how should they now be plunged into poverty and turned to confusion?'

Iodasaph said: 'What is the source of your clothing?'

But he said: 'Our clothing is old and tattered, gathered up from refuse-heaps.'

Iodasaph said: 'Then accept raiment for your companions!'

Balahvar said: 'None of us amasses raiment, for each one puts on only what suffices to conceal the infirmity of the flesh. If a man be waiting for death from eventide, what need has he of the double set of robes which you are wearing?'

Iodasaph said: 'Then how did you come to dress yourself in that sort of apparel?'

Balahvar answered: 'I have put on this apparel just lately to visit you, so that no one should be shocked at the sight of my clothing. Now this instance is like that of a person who has a kinsman in captivity, and enters the enemy's country in disguise to release the prisoner by a stratagem. And I likewise, learning that you were seeking after truth and longing for the gospel message, detected a place meet for sowing; and I came from the country where I dwell and put on this garment which a devout and god-fearing man gave me, and journeyed to you. By the power of Christ you are now delivered from your foes, for I have taught you the precepts of God and His law, and how this world is a harlot and remains not constant in love for any man. But when I reach the place where I donned this garment, I shall take it off there and assume the guise and garb of my companions. But had you seen me in my companions' guise and costume, you would never have wanted to come with me.'

Then he prayed him to show himself in this likeness and garb. So Balahvar took off the robe which he had donned on top. And all his body was dried up and wasted away, and his skin was drawn tightly over his bones, and every joint could be counted. And he was wearing the tattered remains of a sort of hair apron, which hung from his navel half-way down his shins.

When Iodasaph saw this sight of pious austerity, his heart suddenly welled up and he wept exceedingly; and his bowels of compassion were moved and he sobbed like one who sobs over a beloved son, and said: 'Since you will not take me with you, give me this hair garment, and accept another from me, whatever one you please.' So Balahvar acceded to his wish and gave him the hair garment, and himself put on another, old and worn.

But Iodasaph told him that he should accept a new one.

Balahvar said: 'It is not seemly that I should take a new garment in exchange for an old one.'

And he exhorted him and said: 'O king's son I am the servant of Our Lord Jesus Christ, and my mission to you is accomplished, as the Holy Spirit commanded me, for I have expounded all His laws before you. But now I desire to perform the same mission towards other men and seek out fruitful places for me to sow in. On the point of departure, I leave you these guiding rules: Observe before God His command, which He has conveyed to you through me, and fulfil His laws and show yourself worthy before Him. But take care not to transgress against His teachings and fall into the pit of perdition. And I shall beseech God, who brings all good things to fruition, to strengthen you against the assaults of the foe, and grant you wisdom with valour, as well as perseverance, so that your days may be tranquil, and that our enemies the devils may not prevail over you, to make you fall away from the majesty of God. But I am fearful, seeing that you are a king's son and brought up in luxury and ease, lest you may prove inconstant, and stumble away from the path of truth, and lest sins start to assert their power over you.'

Iodasaph said in reply: 'You call me a king's son. Yet I am no king's son, but a slave and son of the immortal King. Through you, God has magnified His benevolence towards me, since you have been for me the instrument of the knowledge of God, and have set me upon the path of truth and saved me from the snares of the devil. Great is the reward I owe you for your kindnesses towards me, and I cannot sufficiently render thanks to you as I ought; however, I place my trust in God, that He will recompense you on my behalf, for to Him belongs the fullness of reward, and He will perform His act of bounty towards you for my sake. If you will abide with me, you are the delight of my soul; and if you depart, let God not cut us off from His grace.' And they took leave of one another, and Balahvar departed to his own abode.

From thenceforward Iodasaph began to fast and pray to God. At the hour when men fall asleep, he would begin to hold vigil; and with tears and groaning he performed his devotions.

But Zandan his tutor fell ill through fear of the king. When the king learnt of his sickness, he sent physicians, that they might diagnose the origin of his malady. When they had made their investigation, they went off and reported to the king: 'O king, this distemper of Zandan's is not the result of any illness, but arises from a state of depression.'

Then he said in his heart: 'There is some worry affecting his spirit. I wonder if anyone can have turned my son away from my faith, and whether this is what is troubling Zandan, my son's tutor?'

So he arose and went to visit him to find out what was paining him, or why he was sorrowful. But when Zandan learnt of the king's arrival, he was disturbed, and came forth into his presence.

And the king said: 'What ails you, Zandan?'

But he replied: 'Live, O king, for ever! A great woe has seized upon me and afflicts me exceedingly and powerfully troubles me, for your son has renounced your faith and espoused that of Christ. Because of this, I am smitten with sickness.'

He said: 'And who has done this?'

But he said: 'Balahvar, whom you dismissed, disguised himself from me, and I failed to recognize him. And he has seduced him.'

And the king was extremely dejected, and returned to the palace. And he summoned a certain counsellor and astrologer, whose name was Rakhis, and said: 'What am I to do? For my son has cut himself off from my faith!'

But he said: 'First, we must discuss and investigate his error. If we cannot persuade him, we will look for some other means.'

Then immediately they went to Iodasaph's quarters, and when they had greeted him, they sat down. And the king said to his son: 'My child, what is this delusion of yours? Tell me!'

But he said: 'It is no delusion, for in truth I am following after Him who created me and gave me birth. It is you who are deluded, for you have abandoned the Creator, and you serve objects which have been created. And if you will listen to me and worship the God who made the heavens and the earth, the sea and all that is therein, for He created sun and moon and stars: if only you will worship that God, then blessings will come both upon you and upon us.'

So he lost hope of convincing him, and said: 'Those philosophers were telling the truth about him when they said: "This child will turn into an adversary of your religion." ' And he got up and went downcast away to his palace.

Then he said to Rakhis: 'What method shall we employ now?'

But he said: 'I know a man in whose company I was educated. Nobody in this country is acquainted with him, and he belongs to our faith and is extremely versed in wisdom. And his name is Nakhor. Let us bring him here, for he greatly resembles Balahvar in complexion and stature. And let us dress him in the robe which Zandan saw Balahvar wearing. But we shall go out on a search for Balahvar, in spite of the fact that we have no chance of finding him. Then we shall tell your son: "We are off to look for your teacher, and if we find him, we will bring him before you." But we shall sally forth, and instead of Balahvar, we will produce Nakhor. Then he can speak to him, saying: "Everything I told you was false, the reason being that I was hostile towards your father." And by this stratagem we shall convert your son to our faith.'

When the king heard this, he was pleased with the words of Rakhis, and they went out to look for Balahvar. And in the course of their journey, at one place they encountered some hermits, servants of God, who bore holy relics hanging at their necks. When they had brought them before the king, he asked them: 'What sort of men are you? And what are those bones you have hanging round your throats?'

But they said: 'We are men who serve God, and therefore we have these relics hung upon us to remind us constantly of death.'

And the king said: 'How do those bones remind you more forcibly of death than do your own conscience and reason? For everyone knows that he is mortal!'

And one of the men said: 'If you were conscious of your mortal nature, then you would not be persecuting the servants of God. For we know and have learnt that you are hunting for Balahvar.'

And Rakhis said to them: 'Where is that charlatan, who has seduced the king's son?'

But the other said: 'It is you who are a devil and a charlatan. The man in question, however, is a companion of ours, adorned with every grace, and girded about with the fear of God.'

And Rakhis said: 'Where is he now?'

But they declared: 'We know not where he is: if he had so desired, then he would have shown himself to you. But you are wasting your efforts, since God is hiding him and you cannot find him. Why are you harrying this brother of ours, who has cast aside temporal glory, and no longer has any concern with it, whereas you do not persecute those who pass their time in partaking of the delights of the world?'

The king said: 'It is because he is deluded, and deludes others too, and prevents them from enjoying the good things and delights which were created for mankind's sake—this is the cause of my wrath against such people, because they bear no love for the good things of the earth.'

The spokesman retorted: 'If this indeed be so, and you desire all men to live in ease, then why do you not share out your good things among all men, seeing that you indulge ostentatiously in every kind of luxury? Then the poor, the hungry and the naked will hasten in from all sides!'

The king said: 'This is because king and slave, duke and commoner are not equal, and also in order that every man shall receive luxury and honour according to his measure.'

The man retorted: 'By this very word of yours, already you have set your own speech at naught! For you are seeking after your own advantage and not that of men. Now if you see fit, I will teach you the reason why you are afire with resentment and filled with evil intent towards those who have quitted the enjoyment of this life.—It is because you foresee the multiplying of the faithful: and when they have multiplied, they will no longer submit to the yoke of the servitude you impose, and therefore you loathe and persecute them.'

And the king said: 'Is there any one of your companions superior to you?'

But the man said: 'No one is either superior or inferior, because we are all one through Jesus Our Lord. However, the world to come is superior to you and your associates!'

Then the king ordered them to be chopped limb from limb and

cast forth upon the roadway. And he told Rakhis to produce Nakhor. So Rakhis went out secretly by night and summoned Nakhor and apprised him of the king's entire scheme, and he instructed him to come out along the road. When it grew light, Rakhis proceeded to the locality where Nakhor was. However, he came walking along the road, and the king told his slaves to enquire who this man was. When they asked him, he said: 'I am Balahvar.' Then they seized him and joyfully brought him before the king. And the king was as glad as if he had found the object of his search, and despatched one of his slaves to inform Iodasaph of the arrest of Balahvar.

When he heard of this, he sighed and began to mourn, and he said within his heart: 'Heaven forbid that he should become frightened of the torture to be inflicted on him by order of my father, and start acting in opposition to me, to make me submit to my father's command!' Thereupon he wept and said: 'O Lord, why didst Thou deliver Thy servant Balahvar into the hands of the impious king? Why didst Thou not hide him from his eyes?'

But the slave was in secret a lover of Christ, and he said: 'O king's son, do not grieve, for this is not Balahvar, but Nakhor, his double.'

And Iodasaph was glad thereat, and glorified God.

Meanwhile, as soon as the slave had gone off to visit the king's son, the king enquired: 'Are you Balahvar, who deluded my son?'

The other said: 'If I am he, then I have rendered no small service to you.'

The king said: 'And what services have you to bring to my notice?'

He said: 'Namely these.—You desire to educate your son, so I have exercised him in the true doctrine, even to the extent of initiating him into the life of the soul; and I have taught him what the holy prophets and apostles proclaimed to us and what God has prepared for those who love Him, for he was an adversary to God and I have reconciled him. Thus he has come to cherish Him, and has rejected your impious ways.'

Then the king said: 'I have no intention of killing you until I have interrogated you fully.' And he mounted his steed and went off to his palace.

The news that the king had seized Balahvar spread abroad. And on the morrow, the king arose and went out to see his son, and said to him: 'My child, no such joy was ever vouchsafed to anyone as was granted to me on account of you. But now you have turned all this joy into sorrow and misery, and darkened the light of my eyes, and you have brought about that very thing which I was warding off for your sake. I was planning that after my death, you should be the heir to my possessions and my realm, but you have ruined my design by falling into that very snare of which I was apprehensive. For I was shielding you from the baneful influences of the world, but through your ignorance and childishness, you have fallen into all those evil ways, opposed my will, abandoned my faith and delivered the tresses of your hair into the hands of false men and seducers who have led you into sorrow and will hurl you into perdition.'

Iodasaph answered his father: 'It was my intent, O king, not to declare my belief in God until my departure from the flesh, so as not to be a harbinger of grief to you. For I said in my heart: "Should I depart from the body before my father in the service of God which I profess, it is well. But if my father should depart before me, let him not pass away grieved owing to my opposition to him. If it be pleasing to Our Lord Jesus Christ, let me go away into the wilderness after my father's death, there to render myself acceptable to the Lord." As it is, I am guiltless before you, since it is you who have made my conduct public.'

When he heard these words, the king cursed him and started to rail against Christ, the True God.

Iodasaph said: 'I know not, O king, for what reason you are sorrowful. Is it for the good thing I have found for myself, or because of my opposition to your will? If you are angry at my finding the good thing, then I shall have to flee away from you, since you have no desire for my welfare. But if you are blaming me for opposing you, and desire my destruction because I have acted against your will, then I pity you for being excluded from those good things which I have won and in which you cannot share, and which are a hundred times loftier than earthly ones, as much so as those stars of heaven you see above. But if you carry your threat into action, then I shall be blessed, for I shall enter beforetime into those good things which the prophets proclaimed, and the apostles confirmed.'

Rakhis said: 'Who knows whether the prophets and apostles spoke the truth?'

He said: 'I know it through the fact that they used to perform signs and miracles which no one else could perform. And these they did by invoking the name of God, in order to impart faith to the whole world.'

And Rakhis continued to enquire into the words of Iodasaph in his father's presence, until at length Rakhis himself acknowledged God and said: 'He is uttering the whole truth, and we are expending fruitless toil in worshipping idols.' And he made his confession before the whole people and declared with a loud voice: 'There is no God upon earth besides the one God who created heaven and earth.' And he professed the entire doctrine of the faith, and began to pray and fast.

However, King Abenes was downcast at the words of Rakhis and exclaimed: 'I acted justly in destroying and expelling those deceivers and charlatans from my country, and I meant to act for the best towards my son. But they corrupted him through his youth and ignorance. Now lo and behold, the chief of the wise, this man Rakhis, has been led astray by him in his turn!'

Iodasaph answered and said: 'You treat me like a child, in spite of the fact that I have come of age and cannot plead my youth as an excuse before Christ. You condemn my good works and are trying to force me to surrender eternal blessings in return for temporal and perishable ones. Know then that there is no comparison between things imperishable and things doomed to perish. As for those boons of yours, you yourself might well take them away from me as a result of some trifling vexation; in any case, the passage of time will sweep away both you and me altogether. But concerning the joy everlasting, the Lord speaks thus: "No one shall take this joy from you".[1]

'The career and life which you chose for me is fair and beautiful but for the fact that it passes speedily away. If one has the courage of purpose to stand fast therein, it is good and desirable. But being devoid of any such ambition, why should I not wish to renounce it so as to receive that life which is most to be desired? Why are you astonished, O king, at my yearning for eternal blessings, and not amazed rather at this attachment of yours to transitory pleasures?

'Now this wretched plight of mine here below is an advantage, as it may enable me to gain eternal life. How could I fail to tire of this world, seeing that it wearies even those who are in love with it? Why should not I be entitled to change, when the world itself involves men in changes of the utmost variety? Or why

[1] John, xvi. 22.

should I rely on its benefits when those benefits are bad? Today it bestows them, and tomorrow takes them away!

'But you have failed to comprehend this, and have risen up against God's law. You show no readiness to cherish His beneficence, although He is merciful and desires the conversion of all mankind. Therefore you will receive retribution for what you have meted out to His slaves and servants.'

Then the king was mollified, and he realised that his scheme was merely inspiring his son's mind even more strongly with the love of God. And he arose and went away to his palace. On the next day he came again, and clasped him to his bosom and embraced his neck and said: 'O son and inmost part of mine, do not imagine that I had any evil intent towards you. What is more, you know the righteousness and justice with which I administer the law towards widows, orphans and paupers, and how I distribute my riches among them. For you are aware how on my frequent encounters with poor folk, orphans, widows and people in stricken circumstances, I never turn aside until I have satisfied their need. How then, my child, could you come to hate my faith and curse my religion? And how could you fail to realise that the devil has seen through your stupidity and weakness and has puffed you up as if you had reached the summit of divine knowledge, and that with this in view, he has laid a snare for you through the tongue of his accomplice Balahvar? How can you presume to judge what is truth for you, and what is error for me? But I am confident, my son, that your heart will give you better counsel, and that greater blessings are yet to be vouchsafed to you by God, and through you, to me. For the tradition of your fathers will prevail upon you.' And all these words he spoke to him in cheerful tones.

But when Iodasaph heard this speech, his heart was fortified and he said: 'O king, since our fathers were worshippers of God, why then did you abandon the faith of your forebears? A fine discourse you have made to me today, while setting a trap for me by your actions! However, your mind's infirmity is grave. We must not expect a rapid cure for it, but it is my duty to seek a remedy. It would not be right for me to address you with any lack of courtesy, for you are my father, and children's respect towards their parents is a very needful thing. At the same time, anyone who speaks to you deceitfully is deficient in loyalty towards you. Now smooth away the agitation from your heart, and examine your own best interests. You must realise that you are soon fated to die and leave all your glory to others. Behold, you see that as soon as death carries men away, others take possession of their treasures. But after some lapse of time, we are all destined for resurrection, and to each will be given according to his works. Hear me now, and ponder in your heart the better course. For there is no one in this world capable of instructing you in what things are best, save certain devout men abiding in the wilderness, who believe in Our Lord Jesus Christ; and they have knowledge of the retribution and the judgement. If you see fit, bring one of them face to face with some who are expert in your faith, and we will hold a disputation: and then truth will be distinguished from falsehood.'

When the king had listened to these words of his son, he was dumbfounded. As he recovered his wits, he began to struggle with his own propensities, but was hard beset by his desires, which reminded him of the pleasures and luxury to which he was accustomed; and his inward voice spoke to him, saying: 'You cannot exist a single day without the things you are used to, and even to overcome this would be a bitter and detestable effort.'

After this, he said to him: 'My son, what you have said has impressed me and converted me to your point of view. Now let us enquire into your words without delay, and investigate them calmly. If they turn out to be true, then they will shine forth all the more in the course of the examination. So I propose to gather the people together and hold a debate in a spirit of equity, and no longer one of violence. And I will command the herald to proclaim an amnesty, that all those who belong to your creed may come to our assembly in order that a just verdict may be reached in the presence of the whole nation, so that you shall not say that I have brought any force to bear. And may our cause be settled on a just basis!'

Then the king gave orders for the assembly of the people, and the idol-worshippers approached. Nakhor, who was feigning to be Balahvar, stood beside the king's son. But not one from among the faithful attended the gathering, except for a certain man who was secretly attached to the faith of Christ: his name was Barakhia, and he was ready to help Balahvar. And the king took his seat upon his throne, but Iodasaph upon the ground, for he had no wish to sit on a throne.

First of all, the king began to address the idol-worshippers and said: 'Behold, you are the heads of this faith, so you must acquit yourselves steadfastly today. If you win, good will your reward be;

but if you lose, know this, that I will break my crown, overturn my throne, shave off the hair of my head and join the ranks of the penitents. And I shall burn your gods and exterminate all you, their acolytes; and your houses shall be pillaged and your children and wives given into bondage.'

Then he turned to his son, and said, pointing to Nakhor: 'There is your teacher. Now let a debate be held in our presence!'

Iodasaph answered: 'O king, you have promulgated a just decree, as befits a monarch.' And to Nakhor he said: 'You know, Balahvar, how you found me amid luxury and delights and called upon me to adopt your creed, and you assured me of your sincere attachment to it. And I abandoned my humility towards the king and rose up against his command, and resigned myself to a life spent in austerity, all owing to fear of the torments which you proclaimed to me. Behold now, the multitude of foes are gathered together, and there is no advocate of ours among them. And you have heard the judgement of the king. But if you have been laying some trap for me, to deprive me of my enjoyments, and if now you are defeated by those people, then be firmly convinced of this, that I shall instantly vent my wrath on your tongue and heart and tear them out with my own hands and cast them to the dogs. This I shall do because you will have made a mockery of a king's son. This oath I utter before God and this whole assembly!'

When Nakhor heard these words, he was afraid and realised that he had fallen into the snare which he had fashioned. And he knew that he could not escape by any stratagem, but only through confessing Christ and by the aid of the creed of Balahvar. So imagining the king to have given up the scheme previously devised, Nakhor opened his mouth and started to denounce the idols and to praise Christ and those who perform His law. Such a pitch of eloquence did his speech attain that even Balahvar could not have equalled his oration against the idol-worshippers.

Thereupon Iodasaph was joyful in spirit, and his face became radiant, and he thanked God who had fortified His religion through the mouth of His adversaries. And the debate between them continued. The king was filled with indignation against Nakhor for the excellence of his speech, but could not rebuke him for shame before the people; and the king said within his heart: 'I have brought this evil upon myself!'

So the king began himself to speak and argue with Nakhor. But Nakhor answered him in forceful terms, whereby he put even the king to confusion. As he was terrified of Iodasaph, he was not in any way intimidated by the king. Night drew on, and victory was not made manifest on either side, because Nakhor wanted to spare the king humiliation. So Iodasaph said to the king: 'Behold, O king, no victory has been made manifest on either side. Act fairly now, and leave my teacher with me, and yours with you.' The king wanted to admonish Nakhor secretly not to oppose him in the course of the debate. However, to please his son he let Nakhor alone and hoped that as a result of their plot, Nakhor for his part would moderate his arguments.

But the king's son said to Nakhor secretly: 'I know this affair of yours: for you are Nakhor. But be glad, for you have striven well today on behalf of God's cause. I have taken you away to protect you from the king's malevolence, because you have put him greatly to shame today, and he wishes you ill. However, we have no desire to avail ourselves of the help of your lips against your will. But if you understand the truth of the matter, you must be aware that your help was from above, otherwise how could you have withstood so great a multitude of people? Come then, take thought, and respond to the summons of God and enter into His faith, take up the Cross and follow Christ!'

Nakhor said to him: 'I am ready, O king's son, to accept what you urge upon me. I believe in one God, and recognize that all things owe their existence to Him. And now I repent of my sins, for He is the Prince of mercy and waits for the conversion of sinners. Rejoice, O king's son, now that you have held fast to His will. And I advise you to honour your father and live together with him in a conciliatory spirit, until God provides a way for you. However, I am ashamed to look your father in the face, since I was brought here to aid him, but have prevented the execution of the plot regarding you, being terrified of you. Now I must flee from your father's face, so let me go and depart into the wilderness. If the Lord wills, I will come again before you at some later time. I believe in the Father, the Son and the Holy Ghost, and this is my confession.'

The king's son gave his permission and bade him go in peace, and Nakhor departed filled with faith. But when the king heard of this, he lost faith even in Nakhor, and postponed the debate with his son. And he began to despise the cult of idols and to treat their acolytes with contempt.

After a little time, the festival day of the idols arrived, and the priests of the idols were afraid lest the king should omit to come and offer a sacrifice to the idols. Therefore they went to Thedma, an idol-worshipper dwelling in the wilderness: and the king and all the people placed great trust in him, for they imagined that the rain and the sunshine were granted to their country as a result of his prayers. And they brought this man to the king, as an ally for their cause.

When he came in before the king, he had no garment upon him besides the ancient piece of hair cloth with which he girded his loins. And when the king saw him coming in towards him, he arose and greeted him and welcomed him cordially. After they had sat down, he said: 'O king, may you live by the power of the idols. For I have heard that you have striven greatly on the idols' behalf, and I am delighted that victory was granted to you.'

But the king said: 'We have received no victory from anywhere! So you must help us as much as you can.'

Thedma said: 'It is fitting first of all to celebrate the festival of the idols, and afterwards to engage the foe. For they are allies in the campaign against the enemy.'

FABLE THE TENTH

The Amorous Wife

The king said: 'Your situation and mine resemble that of a certain warrior who possessed a comely wife. Now the husband was afraid that his wife might become frustrated and commit fornication. Therefore he instructed his wife and said to her: "If you should feel the urge and cannot withstand your flesh, let down the hair of your head. And when I see this, I will fulfil your desire, and you will not fall into sin." One day, enemies approached and there was an alarm; and that champion arrayed himself to go out and fight. But when his wife saw him in his panoply, she was seized with passion and promptly let down her hair. When the champion saw this signal that he had taught her, he turned back and fulfilled his wife's desire. By the time he emerged, the pursuers had already turned the enemy to flight and were returning home, and they reprimanded that warrior for sallying forth too late. But he said to them: "My private foe was battling with me and I have driven him out. And it was he who prevented me from arriving in time."

—Now, Thedma, cure for me the one whom I fondly love. Afterwards, if you allay my disquiet through this, then I will perform the service of the idols.'

Thedma said: 'There is nothing more useful and effective than celebrating the festival of the gods.'

The king said: 'I wonder whether the God against whom we are struggling may not be the truer one. However, if you so wish, then you can go and celebrate it. But I shall remain in doubt until it is revealed to me what is best.'

At this, Thedma was enraged: and he threw down the staff which he held in his hand, tore off the rags which he had wound round his loins and stood naked in front of the king, and said: 'I can easily forsake this stick and these rags, and I am not afraid of the monastic way. There is no existence more austere than my life, since I possess nothing in this world besides the earth on which I crawl along, and the grass on which I nourish myself.'

When the king heard these words, he lost all hope. And he recognized the impotence of their faith, and was minded to confess the one and only God. As he meditated on this, an evil-smelling spirit emerged from his mouth and recalled to him the savours of this world. And he was overcome by his habits and said to Thedma: 'By what means may my son's conversion be effected?'

FABLE THE ELEVENTH

The Youth who had never seen a Woman

He said: 'I heard of a certain king who had a son. And the physicians declared: "If the child sees the sun before he is ten years old, the light of his eyes will be extinguished." So the king hollowed out a cave and placed his son inside. After ten years, he ordered his son to be brought out. And the king commanded to be set before his son those things which he had never seen, so that he should learn the identity of whatever object he might catch sight of. Then the child enquired the name of each separate item. In addition he noticed some women and was fired with passion and enquired: "What are those?" But they said to him: "Those are devils, which ruin men." But the child said: "I have seen nothing more beautiful and more desirable than those devils!"—Now, O king, you too must seek out women to allure him; and as he associates with them, he will forget eternity and be absorbed in the transitory world.'

Now the king possessed a comely woman, a royal princess who had been taken captive, and other maidens who piped and played upon the lyre. And he summoned them all and said to them: 'I can definitely assure you that whichever arouses lust in my son and excites him to fleshly desire, that one among you will I endow with splendid gifts; and I will make her my son's wife, and grant her a queen's estate.' And he told them to remove all his son's male attendants, and appoint those fair women in their stead. When they had done this, each one of these made haste to tempt Iodasaph, and they danced before him and sang his praises with the flute and lyre.

But when he felt the onset of lust, he lit a candle and held his finger to it; and as soon as it was scorched, he withdrew it and said: 'O wretched Iodasaph, if you cannot withstand that flame which you light yourself and may again extinguish, then how will you endure the fire eternal and unquenchable, and how will you suffer the outer darkness? Hold back now from evil and sin!' And in this way he resisted the promptings of his heart.

However, he loved the captive princess dearly for her wisdom and intelligence, and he taught her the faith of Christ. But she said: 'O king's son, if you desire my conversion to your faith, then accede for one year to my desire.'

He answered: 'Suppose I do not survive that long, and death overtakes me, then what would be my comfort?'

But the woman said: 'It would be namely this, that you will have made me into a servant of God; and for this you would be rewarded.'

Iodasaph said: 'That is so, but I should not win the grace of self-denial, like the saints who endured and quenched the furnace of the flesh. Furthermore, I fear the habit of indulgence might entice me into some other enterprise, or that sin might rule me and hurl me into damnation, or that I might be exposed as an enemy of my God and a friend of devils.'

Then the woman said: 'Spend one month with me, or even one night, and I will fulfil all your desire. After all, a small sin like this cannot harm you in any way, for it is I who am taking on the role of temptress.'

Now Iodasaph was favourably disposed towards the maiden's request, because of his wish for her salvation, and also because their lusts would be satisfied. While he was thus inclined he fell asleep, after praying to God that He would instruct him what was for the best. And in his dream he saw the many-coloured delights of paradise, and palaces plastered over with gold, of which the like did not exist in this world. And the angels who accompanied him were saying: 'This is the saints' abode of rest.' And again they led him into hell, and he saw the fearsome torments therein. And they said: 'This is the retribution of sinners.' When he awoke, he surveyed in his mind the beauty of heaven, and then again the bitterness of hell. And he was amazed at the glory of God, and magnified the mercies of Him who had not surrendered him to be hurled into the pit of sin. And he dismissed all those women from his palace.

When his father learnt of this, he came to him and asked what it was that he had seen. So he told him everything he had witnessed, and begged him with tears to let him go into the wilderness.

But when the king heard these words, he was filled with wrath and mortification and said: 'There is no greater evil that can befall me; for if some great king or foeman were to take my son away from me, I could find no consolation except in death. And now I fear the boy is going to run wild and start associating with the hermits. What is more, I am afraid one of my enemies might slay this fair fruit of my inmost parts. Thereby I should be made an object of scorn to my foes; and who will there be in that case to comfort me for this event, which causes me such sorrow and deep grief?'

Thereupon his dignitaries said to him: 'It is not expedient, O king, to permit this offspring of yours to quit your realm like this. If you let sundry people leave your kingdom, then we apprehend that your realm's dissolution may ensue.' And they continued to enlarge on this theme.

So the king and all the leaders of the people decided to give half his kingdom to Iodasaph. And they said to the king: 'If he takes a hand in the business of the world, he will acquire a taste for self-indulgence.' Iodasaph for his part consented to reign, with the idea of being able to revive the faith which his father had suppressed.

The king said to Iodasaph: 'My son, the hope which I cherished for your sake was not of this kind; but you have destroyed it and declared opposition towards me. But paternal affection inclines me in your favour. You do not feel the same distress for my sake as I do for yours, and I realise that I am responsible for my own humiliation. Now behold, I shall fulfil your desire, for the hearts of parents are dominated by love for their offspring. See now, I appoint you king over half my realm. Administer it yourself as you will! Let my enemies not rejoice at my expense, nor let me be completely without posterity from you, lest your extinction make me suffer death before my time comes to pass away! But if you make your kingdom prosper, my soul will not be altogether desolate because of you. And peace be with you.'

Iodasaph said: 'I have paid heed to your words, O king. May God strengthen you with the spirit of peace and grant you that which is best. But I have never entertained any desire for worldly glory, and I deem it preferable for you to let me depart. Even though you may be sad at my absence, I shall be spared from having to disobey your command in order to save my soul from perdition. For my part, I am sorry that I have had to flout your orders: this was not through any intent of disobeying you, but because otherwise I foresaw damnation for my soul. I willingly perform your command now, though not for any love of royal dignity—it is for the sake of obedience to you that I accede to your behest.'

Hearing these words uttered by his son, the king rejoiced greatly. He ordered a herald to be sent out, and summoned all his governors of the people. When they had assembled, he commanded a throne to be set up for his son as well. And he began to address the people and said: 'Whereas all of us adhere to this creed and faith of our conviction and choice, this son of mine desires to follow the creed and faith of our forefathers, and there is a danger that I too may be moved by ancestral tradition.[1] You all know about this boy's conduct, how he has withstood my command, and how I can no longer collaborate with him, since we for our part are in opposition to our forefather's religion. Now I am issuing instructions to hand over to him half of my realm in land and treasure. Let him govern according to whichever faith he pleases!'

Everybody commended the king's solution and proffered

---

[1] As indicated at the opening of this narrative, Christianity was supposed to have been established in India by the ancestors of King Abenes. (Here we have an echo of the legendary mission of the Apostle Thomas.) Abenes is represented as subsequently rejecting the Christian faith and persecuting its followers.

obedience to his authority; and they lauded his design. Then the assembly dispersed. And Iodasaph departed to his own palace amid glory and applause and great honour. But there were certain men from among the Christians, concealing their faith in secret. And all of them came and paid homage to him and wished him success, and they instructed him in the faith and made ready to depart with him into his kingdom.

When Iodasaph was about to set forth to go into his domains, he appeared before his father to bid him farewell, and also to secure the release of all those imprisoned in jail. And he consented to this, and ordered the liberation of all those in confinement. And the king took the royal crown and set it on his head, and gave him abundance of treasure, wished him success, and despatched him into his kingdom, which he had appointed for him.

On his arrival, he distributed generous bounty to the poor and feeble. Then he began to address the people and said: 'No one does it behove to walk in justice so much as a king, for it is his duty to tend his realm with peace and mercy. Accordingly, if God will it, I too will govern this kingdom on the basis of the verdict of equity.' As for the gold and silver vessels which his father had given him for his service, he ordered all these to be sold in foreign lands, and the proceeds distributed among the poor of his country. And he commanded his dukes to judge the widows and orphans, and to administer justice towards everyone. He raised and built up the ruined churches, and set therein priests and deacons, and appointed bishops to direct them. And all the poor were relieved, and no longer was any pauper found begging for alms in that land. Idol-worshippers kept coming and receiving baptism, and good works and the Christian faith were multiplied in the country of King Iodasaph. And everyone with a single voice praised God, the Giver of all good things, and they all rejoiced.

Now when his father observed the decline of his own kingdom and the prosperity of his son's realm, he was greatly weighed down and troubled.

Reports about Iodasaph were noised abroad throughout the entire land, and from all around the multitude of believers flocked together. And he issued instructions to all the lawgivers and priests that no one should exercise authority over them save God. He held them all in high esteem, and maintained all the churches for the glory of God.

On one occasion King Abenes sent men who were idol-worshippers to visit his son, so that they might get to know about his son's doings and policy. When they arrived at the palace, he came out to meet them, as if they had been beloved brethren. And he greeted them with respect and cordiality and entertained them and presented them with great largesse and called upon them to worship God.

But they said: 'O king's son, what think you regarding us, because of those previous actions which we performed at your father's orders? For we have spilt the blood of many.'

Iodasaph said: 'As soon as you shed your religion, you may shed simultaneously any misgivings you entertain on that score. And as soon as you enter into the religion of God, you will enter into peace and joy eternal. For our God is one of peace and love, and with Him is no quest for vengeance, since He is tender and merciful and benevolent, and desires not the death of sinners, but their conversion and repentance.'

And those men returned into the king's presence and informed him of everything which they had heard and seen. Then the king and all his people decided to follow Iodasaph's faith and adopt his creed, and they wrote a letter to this effect. And when the messenger arrived and read out this letter, he was highly delighted, and made the envoys welcome with great honour. On sending them away, he presented them with abundant gifts and wrote to his father in these terms:—

'To the great and pious king, fortunately entered into God's allegiance.—I, the slave and wretch Iodasaph greet you in the Lord's name! Firstly I thank my God, who has not deprived me of my desire, and has made me worthy to look upon your veritable royalty: now indeed you have become a king, whereas previously you were the slave of demons. O beloved father, great now are your favours and gifts to me, and exceedingly great your acts of kindness; but above all you have rejoiced my soul supremely at this time. For everything you had bestowed on me was as nothing before my eyes, since my heart was burnt up on account of your soul's perdition. But now my spirit and mind are lit up through your confession of faith in God, for I have become the son of a pious monarch. Blessed is our God, who has given light to the eyes of your heart! Now I pray you to destroy the temples of the idols, and burn and annihilate all the images, and by burning them to reconcile yourself with God, just as previously you enraged the

Deity against you by burning the men who served God. When you have done this, you will have torn down the wall and barrier of enmity, and you will receive true comfort from God. And may the God of peace be with you for evermore.'

When this letter arrived, the king arose and all the princes with him, and they destroyed all the shrines of the idols and burnt them with fire. Then the king went forth, and all the leaders of the people with him, to the kingdom of his son. And when Iodasaph heard of his coming, he went out to meet him with great joy, and fell down before his father. They greeted each other and went off into the palace and held a great banquet. And Iodasaph presented fine gifts to the king, to his nobles and to all the populace.

Three days later, Iodasaph commanded the priests and prelates to baptise King Abenes and all the people and nobles. And on departing into their own realm, he took with him bishops and priests and deacons; and King Abenes ordered the building of churches throughout all his kingdom and the entire nation was baptised. Then there was great peace and tranquillity in their domain, and everyone magnified God, to whom belongs glory.

But after a little time King Abenes fell ill, and he called his son and committed his whole kingdom into his hands. And he offered blessings and thanks to him for having rendered him worthy of the light of Christ the Lord, and said to him: 'O beloved and cherished son, behold, I am about to depart out of this world, and I suffer greatly and am sorrowful.'

But Iodasaph said: 'Sorrow not, beloved father, for you have come to know Christ the King, and been sealed with the baptism which comes from Him. And now it is an occasion for joy, because you are about to depart into the presence of God, to everlasting delights.'

Abenes answered: 'Do not blame me, my son, for my sorrow, for it is inherent by nature in every soul to feel grief at quitting the flesh, leaving the air and the light, and departing abroad, to a place wherein we know not what ordeals we are to encounter. And I am afraid too because I have greatly angered God my Creator, since I have destroyed many of the saints who will now wreak vengeance upon me; also because I have cursed the true God all the days of my life and praised and glorified idols, and I have no grace in God's sight; and furthermore, because even the time of my repentance has been cut short.'

Iodasaph answered and said: 'Have no care, O king, but be

glad, because you are going before a gracious and much forgiving Sovereign, who has granted even those of the eleventh hour the same reward as those of the first, for nothing is lacking in God's mercies; neither does the Lord judge according to the way of men, for His compassion prevails over this sinful world. What is more, the light and the airy breezes of this world cannot compare with the light and the air of His glory, of which the faithful shall be made worthy, and no one may put on the imperishable raiment until he has endured the perishing of the flesh. Know too that a little repentance wipes out a multitude of sins, for God lavishes His mercies upon those that fear Him.'

At this the king became steadfast; and he found consolation in these words and was cheered in spirit from out of his woe. And he said: 'May God of His bounty grant you, my son, the supreme reward, even exceeding the bounds of your hopes. For I was doomed and you saved me, I was a prisoner and you freed me, and I was a foe and you reconciled me to God. Now I exhort you to walk virtuously before God and complete your days in a way that is pleasing to him; let not the pomp of kingship cut you off from the love of God, seeing that all this is but shadowy and transitory. Where now is the fearsome terror of my majesty, or the multitude of hosts and the courage of my valiant knights, or my countless treasures which I have heaped up for myself? How shall they come and deliver me from my pall-bearers? Now, my son, I too exhort you, just as you have exhorted me, and I admonish you, just as you have admonished me, to despise the world and all that is in the world, until you yourself find God. And cause me to be remembered in your prayers, O my son!'—When he had pronounced these words, he saw angels clad in light, and he made the sign of the Cross over himself and delivered up his spirit.

But Iodasaph, the king's son, buried his body, as though it had been that of a common man. And he raised his hands up towards heaven and directed his gaze aloft and said: 'I thank Thee, O Lord my God, King of glory, who didst convert this errant slave of Thine, and didst not cast him forth into the torments of hell, and didst make him worthy of the light of Thy face. Welcome him, O Lord, and cherish him like the prodigal son and allot his soul a place among the just and the saints. And remember not the injuries which he inflicted upon Thy slaves, for Thou art merciful and omnipotent.'

Forty days long he stood upon the grave, and for all that time he made sacrifice with tears towards God. After this, he summoned all the prelates, priests and deacons, and distributed among them much treasure and bade them offer sacrifice and prayer for King Abenes; and likewise he made a distribution among the poor, the widows and the orphans. Then he took his seat upon his throne and commanded his grandees also to be seated. And he said: 'Behold, King Abenes my father has found rest, just like anyone from among the poor folk, and no one could help him and save him from the hands of death; and this day must come upon each one of us also. You know what was my personal desire: although I was powerless to resist my father, I no longer have any excuse now before God for not fulfilling my promise to join the number of the monks and strictly to adhere to their way of life. So do you choose for yourselves a king to guide you in the will of God. Behold, through the power of Christ, no foe or adversary remains, and our realm is in a calm and tranquil state!'

But when they had listened to these words, they arose and said all with one voice: 'Let this not be, O king; rather let us perish than that this should come to pass!' Whereupon their voices grew louder and louder, until a tumult ensued.

Seeing that they refused him permission, Iodasaph determined to get away secretly. So he summoned Barakhia, whom we have mentioned earlier as having assisted Nakhor on that day when the king held the debate; and he was a kinsman of Iodasaph. And he said to him: 'A man has need of a kinsman in the day of trouble. Accept now a charter addressed to the people and to my princes concerning your accession to the throne. It is my desire to depart and join the brethren, and to serve Christ in their company.'

Barakhia answered: 'You have not made a fair decision, O king, for it is written: "Love thy neighbour as thyself." You, however, have chosen the better thing, and intend to ruin me! If it is preferable to quit the transitory world and seek after the eternal, away then, and let us both depart.'

When Iodasaph had listened to Barakhia's words, he recognized the justice of them and made no answer. But one night, he wrote out and set his hand to a charter addressed to the dukes and the people, declaring: 'To Barakhia belongs the royal authority', and left it upon his couch. And he arose and girded his loins with the hair garment which he had received from Balahvar, and went out by stealth.

But Barakhia learnt of this, and informed the other princes.

So they set out in swift pursuit and caught up with him and carried him with them and said: 'If you forsake so great a multitude without a leader, and supposing strife and tumults arise, or they turn again to the idols, will you not be held to account for all those many souls who abide in your kingdom?'

But he said: 'The lips which lie not declare: "What is a man profited if he shall gain the whole world, and lose his own soul? Or what shall a man give in exchange for his soul?"[1] Now take note that I am firmly resolved to go and join the company of those in whom God is well pleased. But do you seek a king for yourselves.'

Then they laid their hands on Barakhia, to make him king. But he began to weep and refused to consent. However, he could not prevail against the people, and most of all, against Iodasaph. So Iodasaph took up the seal of office, and placed it in Barakhia's hand, and set the crown upon his head, and wished him success in his reign. And he raised his hands aloft and said: 'Blessed art Thou, O Lord, who didst save Thine unworthy slave and didst bring me to hear Thy message, and didst save my soul from desolation through the conversion of my father.—Make manifest now Thy benevolence, and help Barakhia, this brother of mine, that he may walk before Thee and all the people in a manner worthy and pleasing to Thee.'

And when he had addressed many such supplications to God, he removed his hands from Barakhia's shoulders. Then he turned to Barakhia and said: 'I give you this exhortation and testament in the presence of God and of the entire nation. Let me not be exposed to blame through any conduct of yours. Just as you knew God before I did and served Him with a quiet spirit, strive now more zealously than I and make your virtue manifest to God. Harbour no malice against anyone, nor suffer your intellect to be put out of joint by the pomp of your throne. Accept no corrupt gifts, nor rejoice at a foe's discomfiture. Let not your mind be inflamed for the sake of anger, nor look on anyone with the eye of wrath. Inflict no evil on anybody for your own advantage, but only for God's cause. Turn the poor not away empty. These precepts I give you, and if you reject them, may God hold you to account, for He is the beginning and the end of every deed. Act towards all men as you desire them to act towards you; for a good friend is one whom not the wine-cup, but tribulation will rally to you. Love has no boundary; one eye has need of another, for it can see

---

[1] Matthew, xvi. 26.

everything, but itself it cannot see. Should an evil spirit pester you and urge you to commit evil, say to yourself: "Anyone can see through that!" and he will retire back again in shame. But if you go astray, then summon a sagacious person, and he will cure your error.'

When he had completed his discourse of instruction, he arose and girt himself once more with the garment given him by Balahvar, and departed immediately into the desert. But everybody who heard the news about him was amazed at this conduct of Iodasaph, and with tears they all glorified God.

But God tested his spirit all the more, in that it was not until two years later that he discovered Balahvar his teacher upon a certain mountain. And when they saw each other, they embraced one another's necks, exchanged joyous greetings and wept and kissed each other. After they had sat down, Iodasaph told him everything that had happened. And he gave thanks to God, who had made fruitful His seed, which He had sown on good ground.

Then Balahvar revealed that he himself was about to depart from the flesh. Iodasaph began once more to weep, and kept saying to him: 'Do not leave me, spiritual father, prodigal son that I am.'

But he said to him: 'Be not alarmed, my child, for I shall beseech the Lord soon to bear you away to that abode of rest which you have seen.' On uttering these words, Balahvar's face was lit up and he passed away.

Iodasaph laid the corpse of our holy father Balahvar in the grotto wherein he used to dwell. And he sank into deep sorrow. And when he had fallen into a light slumber, he saw in a dream certain men radiant with light, having crowns adorned with garnet stones and gems and saying: 'These crowns are for those whom you have brought to God by your teaching.' They had two others brighter still, and said to him: 'One of these is yours, in return for the feats which you have undertaken, and one is for your father, who has been converted to God.'

Iodasaph answered: 'And what comparison can there be between one who has merely repented, and one who has striven?'

Then Balahvar appeared to him and said: 'Remember, O king's son, what I once told you, namely that when you grew rich, you would have no desire to give anything to your neighbour. And now you are even envious of your own father!' And Iodasaph awoke and was radiant and fortified in spirit.

After some little time Iodasaph too passed away. And one of the hermits abode nearby them; and he came and laid his corpse by the body of Balahvar, and went into the presence of King Barakhia and told him what had taken place. Then he went forth with the people and the priests and bore away the holy relics of Iodasaph and Balahvar, and buried them in a golden urn. Over this he built a church consecrated in the name of the Father, the Son and the Holy Ghost, to whom belongs glory now and from eternity to eternity, Amen.

Whoever comes thither with faith is cured from any disease. And we too must beseech God that through their prayers, we may be delivered from eternal torment: and let us magnify God, to whom belong glory, honour and worship for all eternity, Amen.

FURTHER FABLES OF BALAHVAR

Note: These three apologues are taken from the original, longer Georgian recension of the legend, *The Life of the Blessed Iodasaph,* contained in Jerusalem Ms. No. 140, fols. 40v.-45r.; they fit into the narrative between the fables 'The King for One Year' and 'The King and the Happy Poor Couple'.

Dogs and Carrion

Balahvar said: 'Seekers after worldly bliss, however envious and hostile they may be to one another, yet confine their enmity to transitory matters. Towards the believers who serve Christ Our God, however, they behave like dogs of various hues, gathered together from divers places and crowding round some carrion and biting at each other. But as soon as they catch sight of a wayfarer passing by, they stop snapping at each other and all with one accord co-operate in attacking him, for they imagine this man to be coming along with designs on their carrion. This idea of theirs arises from their greed and gluttony. As soon as they notice that man's alien presence among them, they make common cause against him, although they were previously at enmity; and they fail to realise that this carrion of theirs is quite valueless to him.

'Such are the lovers of this world, who have chosen it in preference to paradise. They devour one another and shed their blood for its sake; and in this occupation they pass their days, engrossed in the quest after worldly honour and glory, the deathly obsession of which constantly dwells within their hearts. But when they observe those people who are foes to this world and have no care other than to free themselves from it and have no share in their worldly ambitions, then they imagine those persons are setting a trap for them with ulterior motive; for they attribute to the believers in Christ their own treacherous mentality. This is why they conspire together to maintain enmity towards us; they have adopted this attitude because of their lack of understanding.'

Physician and Patient

Iodasaph said to Balahvar: 'Put your words into practice, and begin to proclaim the message of salvation!'

Balahvar replied: 'When a skilled physician sees a body deranged by grievous ailments and wishes to restore it to health, he does not attempt to build up the flesh by gorging it with food and drink. For he knows that if food and drink were absorbed, they would disagree with the system and harm the body rather than doing it any good. But those through whom God in His providence operates the conquest of disease will rather impose a regime and administer medicine.

'As soon as the distemper and the corrupt humour have been expelled through God's grace, then it is that they will nourish the patient with food and drink; and straightway the palate will acquire a relish for good cheer, and he whose death God wishes to avert will be restored to health.'

The Sun of Wisdom

Iodasaph said: 'What is that wisdom which is praised for its excellence and perfection and filled with every honourable power? And how is it that not everyone benefits from it?'

The holy Balahvar said: 'The image of that wisdom resembles the sun, which shines upon all mankind, great and small alike; no one is debarred from deriving benefit from it, nor is anyone who so wishes hindered from enjoying its warmth or stretching out his hands towards its radiance. But if anyone does not desire to enjoy it, the sun is not to blame. The same applies to wisdom among men until the day of the resurrection, for it is just as readily accessible as the sunlight.

'However, men surpass one another in this, just as one jewel is worth many hundred shillings (*dangi*) and another two shillings. But whoever shall seek after wisdom and find it and shall cherish that spiritual wisdom, fulfilling it not with lip-service only but in deed, that man shall be like a gem of great price; and if someone shall fail to discover that great jewel, then even a little one, however insignificant, is not without value.'

SELECT BIBLIOGRAPHY

Note: This list is necessarily confined to works with a bearing on the oriental origins of the Barlaam and Ioasaph romance, or relating to the Georgian text translated in this volume. No attempt is made to follow the tale's later diffusion in Western European and Slavonic literatures.

Ilia Abuladze, edit. *Sibrdzne Balahvarisi* ('The Wisdom of Balahvar'), Tiflis, 1937.
Prosper Alfaric. *Les écritures manichéennes*, 2 vols., Paris, 1918-19.
—'La vie chrétienne du Bouddha' in *Journal Asiatique*, 1917, pp. 269-88.
Aśvaghoṣa. *The Buddhacarita, or, Acts of the Buddha*, edit. and trans. by E. H. Johnston, 2 vols., Calcutta, 1935-6.
—'The Buddha's mission and last journey', trans. Johnston, in *Acta Orientalia*, XV, Leiden, 1937.
W. Bang. 'Manichäische Erzähler' in *Le Muséon*, XLIV, 1931, pp. 1-36.
Al-Bīrūnī. *The Chronology of Ancient Nations*, trans. C. E. Sachau, London, 1879.
Carl Brockelmann. *Geschichte der arabischen Litteratur*, Weimar and Leiden, 1898-1949.
E. G. Browne. 'Some Account of the Arabic work . . . which treats of the Persian Kings' in *Journal of the Royal Asiatic Society*, 1900, pp. 195-259.
E. A. Wallis Budge, Sir, edit. and trans. *Baralâm and Yewâsef* (Ethiopic text and trans.), 2 vols., Cambridge, 1923.
F. C. Burkitt. *The Religion of the Manichees*, Cambridge, 1925.
Victor Chauvin. *Bibliographie des ouvrages arabes*, tom. 3, Liége & Leipzig, 1898.
F. C. Conybeare. 'The Barlaam and Josaphat Legend in the Ancient Georgian and Armenian Literatures' in *Transactions of the Folk-Lore Society*, VII, No. 2, June, 1896.
Franz Dölger. *Der griechische Barlaam-Roman ein Werk des H. Johannes von Damaskos*, Ettal, 1953. (See reviews by Glanville Downey in *Speculum*, XXXI, 1956, pp. 165-8; F. Halkin in *Analecta Bollandiana*, LXXI, 1953, pp. 475-80.)
H. T. Francis and E. J. Thomas. *Jātaka Tales*, Cambridge, 1916.
Ignaz Goldziher. *Vorlesungen über den Islam*, 2nd edition, revised by F. Babinger, Heidelberg, 1925.
J. Rendel Harris and J. Armitage Robinson. *The Apology of Aristides*, Cambridge, 1891. (Texts and Studies, Vol. I, No. 1.)

W. B. Henning. *Ein Manichäisches Bet- und Beichtbuch*, Berlin, 1937. (Abhandlungen der Preussischen Akademie der Wissenschaften, 1936, Phil.-hist. Klasse, Nr. 10, Einzelausgabe.)
—'Sogdian Tales' in *Bulletin of the School of Oriental and African Studies, London University*, XI, Pt. 3, 1945.
F. Hommel. 'Die älteste arabische Barlaam-Version' in *Verhandlungen des VII. Internationalen Orientalisten-Congresses, Semitische Section*, Vienna, 1888, pp. 115-65.
Joseph Jacobs. *Barlaam and Josaphat*, London, 1896.
I. A. Javakhishvili (Javakhov), trans. 'Mudrost' Balavara' in *Zapiski Vostochnogo Otdeleniya Imp. Russkogo Arkheologicheskogo Obshchestva*, XI, St. Petersburg, 1897-8, pp. 1-48.
J. J. Jones, trans. *The Mahāvastu*, 3 vols., London, 1949-56. (Sacred Books of the Buddhists.)
M. Kakhadze. *K'art'velebi Bizantiis politikursa da kulturul tskhovrebashi* ('Georgians in the political and cultural life of Byzantium'), Tiflis, 1954.
K. S. Kekelidze. *Dzveli k'art'uli mdserlobis istoria* ('History of ancient Georgian literature'), 3rd edition, Tiflis, 1951.
A. S. Khakhanashvili (Khakhanov). *Balhvar i Iodasaf*, Moscow, 1902. (Trudy po Vostokovedeniyu, fasc. 9.)
Geronti K'ik'odze. 'Sibrdzne Balavarisa. Dzveli da akhali shenishvnebi' ('The Wisdom of Balavar. Old and new observations') in *Literaturuli dziebani*, II, Tiflis, 1944, pp. 173-80.
A. E. Krymsky. *Aban al-Lahiqi, le Zindiq (env. 750-815)*, with an appendix: 'Barlaam et Joasaph: Essai littéraire-historique', Moscow, 1913. (Trudy po Vostokovedeniyu, fasc. 37. In Russian.)
E. Kuhn. 'Barlaam und Joasaph. Eine bibliographisch-literargeschichtliche Studie' in *Abhandlungen der Bayerischen Akad. der Wissenschaften, Philosophisch-philologische Klasse*, XX, Munich, 1894.
D. M. Lang. *Lives and Legends of the Georgian Saints*, London, 1956. (Ethical and Religious Classics of East and West.)
—'St. Euthymius the Georgian and the Barlaam and Ioasaph Romance' in *Bulletin of the School of Oriental and African Studies*, XVII, Pt. 2, 1955.
A. von Le Coq. 'Ein christliches und ein manichäisches Manuskriptfragment in türkischer Sprache aus Turfan (Chinesisch-Turkistan)' in *Sitzungsberichte der Königlich Preussischen Akad. der Wissenschaften, Phil.-hist. Klasse*, 1909, No. XLVIII, pp. 1202-18.
J. Leroy. 'Un nouveau manuscrit arabe-chrétien illustré du Roman de Barlaam et Joasaph' in *Syria*, XXXII, 1955.
Raoul Manselli. 'The Legend of Barlaam and Joasaph in Byzantium and in the Romance Europe' in *East and West*, VII, No. 4, Rome, 1957, pp. 331-40.
N. Y. Marr. 'Armyansko-gruzinskie materialy dlya istorii Dushepolez-

noy Povesti o Varlaame i Ioasafe' in *Zapiski Vostochnogo Otdeleniya Imp. Russkogo Arkheologicheskogo Obshchestva*, XI, 1897-8, pp. 49-78.
—'Mudrost' Balavara, gruzinskaya versiya Dushepoleznoy Istorii o Varlaame i Ioasafe', *ibid.*, III, 1889, pp. 223-60.
R. A. Nicholson. *A Literary History of the Arabs*, revised edition, Cambridge, 1941.
Shalva Nutsubidze. *K proiskhozhdeniyu grecheskogo romana Varlaam i Ioasaf*, Tiflis, 1956.
—'K'art'uli literaturisa da kulturis sakit'khebi t'anamedrove dasavlur metsnierebashi' ('Questions of Georgian literature and culture in contemporary Western scholarship') in *Mnat'obi*, No. 3, March, 1956, pp. 144-54.
—*K'art'uli p'ilosop'iis istoria* ('History of Georgian Philosophy'), vol. I, Tiflis, 1956.
S. von Oldenburg. 'Nachtrag zu W. Radloff, Alttürkische Studien VI' in *Izvestiya Imp. Akademii Nauk*, 6th series, tom. VI, St. Petersburg, 1912, pp. 779-82.
—'Persidsky izvod povesti o Varlaame i Ioasafe' in *Zapiski Vostochnogo Otdeleniya Imp. Russkogo Arkheologicheskogo Obshchestva*, IV, 1890, pp. 229-65.
Paul Peeters. 'La première traduction latine de "Barlaam et Joasaph" et son original grec' in *Analecta Bollandiana*, XLIX, 1931, pp. 276-312.
—*Le tréfonds oriental de l'hagiographie byzantine*, Brussels, 1950. (Subsidia Hagiographica, No. 26.)
Simon Qaukhchishvili. 'Akhali varianti k'art'uli romanisa Sibrdzne Balavarisi' ('A new variant of the Georgian romance The Wisdom of Balavar') in *Mnat'obi*, No. 8, August, 1956, pp. 176-8.
E. Rehatsek, trans. 'The Book of the King's Son and the Ascetic' in *Journal of the Royal Asiatic Society*, 1890, pp. 119-55.
T. W. Rhys Davids, trans. *Buddhist Birth-Stories (Jataka Tales)*, revised edition, London, 1925.
—*The Questions of King Milinda*, 2 vols., Oxford, 1890-94. (Sacred Books of the East, vols. XXXV-XXXVI.)
Viktor R. Rosen, Baron, trans. *Povest' o Varlaame pustynnike i Iosafe tsareviche indiyskom*, translated from the Bombay Arabic version and published posthumously under the editorship of I. Yu. Krachkovsky, Moscow, 1947.
J. Sonet. *Le Roman de Barlaam et Josaphat*, Louvain, 1949. (Université de Louvain, Recueil de travaux d'histoire et de philologie, sér. 3, fasc. 33.)
M. Steinschneider. *Die hebraeischen Übersetzungen des Mittelalters*, Berlin, 1893.
Michael Tarchnišvili. *Geschichte der kirchlichen georgischen Literatur*, bearbeitet... in Verbindung mit Dr. Julius Assfalg, Vatican City, 1955. (Studi e Testi, vol. 185.)

Sirarpie Ter Nersesean. *L'illustration du Roman de Barlaam et Joasaph*, Paris, 1937.

Constantino Vona. *L'Apologia di Aristide*, Rome, 1950.

Nathan Weisslovits, *Prinz und Derwisch*. Mit einem Anhang von Dr. Fritz Hommel, Munich, 1890.

F. Weller. 'Zwei zentralasiatische Fragmente des Buddhacarita' in *Abhandlungen der Sächsischen Akademie der Wissenschaften, Phil.-hist. Klasse*, Band XLVI, Heft 4, Berlin, 1953.

M. Winternitz. *A History of Indian Literature*, vol. II, Calcutta, 1933.

R. L. Wolff. 'The Apology of Aristides—A Re-examination' in *Harvard Theological Review*, XXX, 1937, pp. 233-47.

—'Barlaam and Ioasaph' in *Harvard Theological Review*, XXXII, 1939, pp. 131-9.

G. R. Woodward and H. Mattingly, edit. and trans. *Barlaam and Ioasaph*, London, 1914. (Loeb Classical Library.)

Sir H. Yule and H. Cordier, trans. *The Book of Ser Marco Polo*, 3rd. edition, 3 vols., London, 1926.

R. C. Zaehner. *The Teachings of the Magi*, London, 1956. (Ethical and Religious Classics of East and West.)

H. Zotenberg. 'Notice sur le livre de Barlaam et Joasaph' in *Notices et extraits des mss. de la Bibliothèque Nationale*, XXVIII, Paris, 1886.

POSTSCRIPT

Mr. Graves, Mr. Podro and the Kashmir Shrine

The 'Ahmadiyya Movement in Islam' is well-known to English railway travellers for its conspicuous mosque at Woking. Concerning the movement's founder, Mirza Ghulam Ahmad of Qadiyan (1839-1908), Sir Francis Younghusband wrote in his *Kashmir*, pp. 129-30:—

'There lately died in the Punjab the founder of a curious sect, who maintained that he was both the Messiah of the Jews and the Mahdi of the Mohamedans; that Christ had never really died upon the Cross, but had been let down . . . and that He had come to Kashmir and was buried at Srinagar. It is a curious theory, and was worked out by the founder of the Quadiani sect in much detail. There resided in Kashmir some 1900 years ago a saint of the name of Yus Asaf, who preached in parables and used many of the same parables as Christ used, as, for instance, the parable of the Sower. His tomb is in Srinagar, and the theory of this founder of the Quadiani sect is that Yus Asaf and Jesus are one and the same person.'

The present book was virtually complete when Mr. Robert Graves and Mr. Joshua Podro brought out their monograph, *Jesus in Rome: A Historical Conjecture* (London, Cassell, 1957), in the 5th chapter of which they examine with due caution this legend of Christ's tomb at Srinagar, and its ramifications in Ahmadi tradition.

Even a superficial reading of the sources quoted by Mr. Graves and Mr. Podro, however, suffices to show that they have no possible bearing on the life of Christ, but are simply a reflection of the Muslim story of Gautama Buddha as transmitted in the Arabic 'Book of Balauhar and Budhasaf', the prototype of the Christian Barlaam and Josaphat legend.

We have already tried to show (pp. 29, 39, above) how confusion of diacritical markings in Arabic turned Budhasaf (Bodhisattva) into Yudasaf and even Yuzasaf. Furthermore, the 'Book of Balauhar and Budhasaf' makes the Buddha die in Kashmir, doubtless through confusion with Kusinara where he is in fact reputed to have passed away. The Kashmir story gives Yus Asaf a disciple called Ba'bid; this is the Ababid of 'Balauhar and Budhasaf', the Ananda of Buddhist tradition.

To make all this clear, we quote from the conclusion of the Bombay Arabic edition of the 'Book of Balauhar and Budhasaf', pp. 285-6, corresponding to pp. 182-3 of Rosen's translation:—

'And he (Budhasaf) reached Kashmir (i.e., Kusinara), and this was the most remote place in which he ministered, and there the end of his life overtook him. And he left the world, bequeathing his heritage to a certain disciple, Ababid (i.e., Ananda) by name, who served him and accompanied him; he was a man perfect in all his doings. And he exhorted him and said to him: "I have discovered and cherished and adorned a shrine and set therein lamps for the departed; I have gathered together the flock of the true faith which was scattered and to which I was sent. And now there draws nigh my ascension from the world, and the separation of my soul from the body. Observe therefore the commandments given to you and do not diverge from the truth, but hold fast to it with gratitude.—And let Ababid be the leader." Afterwards he commanded Ababid to smooth out a place for him, then he stretched out his legs and lay down; and he turned his head towards the north and his face to the east, and then he died.'

An almost identical account of the Buddha's death is given by Ibn Bābūya (see Oldenburg's summary, pp. 250-51), where the Buddha's name occurs as Yudhasaf; this same passage turns up practically verbatim among the lore on the Kashmir Yus Asaf garnered by Mr. Graves and Mr. Podro. As for the parable of the Sower, this occurs in the earliest Arabic non-Christian versions of the Budhasaf or Bodhisattva story, and may, as we suggested, have previously been introduced into the story by the Manichaeans.

At any rate, the re-importation into formerly Buddhist Kashmir of a Muslim cult of the Buddha is another curious episode in the history of the Barlaam and Josaphat legend; Mr. Graves and Mr. Podro deserve thanks for bringing its obscure elements into the light of day.

INDEX

Ababid, 130
Abān al-Lāḥiqī, 34
Abasgians, 60
'Abbāsid caliphs, 31-2, 41
Abenes (Abenner), 11, 21, 45-6, 51-6, 69-75, 100-19
Abo, St., 41-2
Abu'l-'Atāhiya, 30
Abū-Manṣūr, al-Baghdādī, 29
Abuladze, I., 6
Acts of the Apostles, 57
Adharwān, 34
Adysh Gospels, 49
Ahlwardt, W., 35
Ahmadiyya Movement in Islam, 129
Ahwaz, 33
Alamino, 43
Alexander the Great, 24, 33
Ananda, 130
Antioch, 42-3
Antiochus Strategus, 43
Antoninus Pius, emperor, 58
Antony Rawaḥ, 43
Arabs, Arabic, 5, 12, 16, 21, 26, 28-56, 64, 129-30
Araches, *see* Rakhis
Ardashir, 34
Aristides, Apology of, 55, 58
Armenia, Armenians, 12, 40-1, 58
Armenian Church, 41
Asita, 13
Aśvaghoṣa, 13, 26
Athanasius of Alexandria, St., 57
Athanasius the Athonite, St., 59, 63
Athos, Mount, 11, 43, 58-9, 62-4

Ba'bid, *see* Ababid
Bābūya, Ibn, 28, 34-5, 130
Babylonia, 25
Bachkovo, 43
Bactria, 24
Baghdad, 29, 31, 34, 41-2, 49, 64
Bahram I, king, 24
al-Bahwan, 39
Balahvar, *see* Barlaam and Ioasaph
Balauhar and Budhasaf, Book of, 26, 32-56, 129-30

Balaver (Balahvar), 5
Balkans, 43
Bang, W., 27
Barakhia (Barachias), 22, 48, 55-6, 107, 119-22
Bardaisan, 24, 29, 32
Barlaam and Ioasaph (Balahvar and Iodasaph), 5, 11-17, 22-3, 25-9, 32, 34, 38, 40, 43-64, 69-124, 129-30
Barlaam of Antioch, St., 11, 53, 56
Barlaam, St., Monastery of, 42
Baronius, 11
Basham, A. L., 17
Basil, St., 45, 57
Basil I, emperor, 43
Basra, 28, 36
Berlin, 26-7, 35
Bethlehem, 42
Bidpai, fables of, 31
al-Bīrūnī, 25, 27
Black Mountain, 42
Blake, R. P., 44
Bo-Tree, 14
Bodhisattva, 5, 11-23, 25, 27-9, 32-9, 49, 51-5, 64, 129-30
Bolaiti (Bolayt), 45, 51, 69
Bombay, 32, 35, 46, 49
Boyce, Mary, 25
Brahmins, 13, 24, 30
British Museum, 6, 33, 35
Brothers of Purity, 36-8
Brough, J., 15, 30
Browne, E. G., 33
Buddha, Gautama, 5-6, 12-25, 31-2, 64, 129-30
Buddha-carita, 13-14, 17-22, 26
Budhasaf, *see* Bodhisattva
Bukhara, 24
Bulgaria, 43
Byzantium, 40-3, 56, 59, 62-3

Calliopius, St., 42
Cambridge, 33
Caspian Sea, 41
Castana Monastery, 42
Catherine of Alexandria, St., 42

Caucasus, 41, 43, 64
Caxton, W., 12
Ceylon, 13, 39, 45, 49, 52
Chalcedon, 41
Chaldaeans, 58
Chandaka, 14, 27-8
Chariton, Monastery of St., 42
Chauvin, V., 36
China, Chinese, 13, 25, 27
Chisdai, Ibn, 38
Chita, the Georgian, 44
Clement of Alexandria, St., 24
Constantine the Great, 41
Constantine Monomachus, 60
Constantinople, 42-3, 58-63
Cosmas and Damian, Saints, 43
Crania Lavra, 43
Cross, Monastery of the, 11, 42-5
Cyprus, 43, 63
Cyril of Jerusalem, St., 57

Damascus, 31, 41
David Kuropalates, 62
David, the translator, 43
devas, 14
Diocletian, 11, 56
Diogo do Couto, 12
Downey, G., 57
Dutch, 12

Egyptians, 58
Elkesaites, 24
Escurial, 62
Ethiopians, Ethiopic, 11-12, 40, 59
Europe, 5, 12
Euthymius the Athonite, St., 5, 43, 45, 56-64

Al-farq bain al-firaq, 29
Farrukhān, king, 33
Ficus religiosa, 14
Fihrist, 32, 34-5
Flügel, G., 32
Four Omens, the, 13-14, 27
French, 12

Gems, the Three, 16
George the Hagiorite, St., 11, 45, 61-3, 69

Georgia, Georgians, 5-6, 11, 40-64
Georgian Church, 41-3, 61
German, 12, 38
German Oriental Society, 35
Gnostic philosophers, 24, 29
Goldziher, Ignaz, 30-1
Golgotha, Mount, 42
Graves, Robert, 129-30
Great Renunciation, the, 5, 14, 16
Greek literature, 40
Greek Orthodox Church, 41, 61-2
Greek Patriarchal Library, Jerusalem, 5-6, 42
Greek philosophy, 36
Greek religion, ancient, 58
Gregory of Nazianzus, St., 57
Gregory Bakuriani, 43

Hadrian, emperor, 58
Halkin, Father F., 58, 62
Halle, 35, 38, 47
Harrān, 28
Harun al-Rashid, 34
Harvard University, 46
Hebrew, 38
Heliogabalus, emperor, 24
Henning, W. B., 25
Hermes, 37
Hilarion the Iberian, St., 42-3, 63
Hindus, 27, 34
Holy Cross Monastery, 11, 42-5
Holy Virgin, Cloister of the, 43
Hommel, F., 35
Horeb, Mount, 42

Iberia (Georgia), 41
Ibrāhīm b. Adham, 31
Imam, the Hidden, 34
India, Indians, 11-26, 29-31, 35, 37, 39, 45, 51-5, 58, 60, 62, 69
Indra, 17
Ingoroqva, P., 61
Ioasaph, St., *see* Barlaam and Ioasaph
Iodasaph, St., *see* Barlaam and Ioasaph
Iran, Iranians, 27-32, 37
Iraq, 28, 33
Isaac, Father, 69
Islam, 30-8, 41
Ismāʿīlī sect, 37
Italian, 12
Iviron Monastery, 11, 43, 59, 62

Jacobs, J., 5, 36, 40
Jacobus de Voragine, 11, 47
Janaysar, king, 39, 46
Jātaka tales, 13, 31
Jerome, St., 58
Jerusalem, 5–6, 11, 23, 38, 42–55, 58–9, 62–3, 123
Jews, 58, 129
John the Athonite, St., 43, 62
John Chrysostom, St., 53, 56–7
John Climacus, St., 57
John of Damascus, St., 11–12, 23, 57–62
John the Monk, of St. Saba, 59–60
John Sabanisdze, 41
Johnston, E. H., 14, 17
Jones, J. J., 14
Joppa, 69
Josaphat, St., *see* Barlaam and Ioasaph
Josephus, 57
Journal des Débats, 12
Justinian I, emperor, 42

Kalila wa Dimna, 31, 34, 37
Kaniṣka, king, 13
Kaṇṭhaka, the Buddha's horse, 14, 27
Kapilavastu, 13, 15, 39
Kashgar, 27
Kashmir, 129–30
Kekelidze, K., 63
Khuzistan, 33
King's Son and the Ascetic, The, 38
Kitāb al-Budd, 32, 35–6
Kitāb Būdhāsaf mufrad, 32–4
Klarjo-Meskhian synaxary, 61
Koṇḍañña, 13
Krachkovsky, I., 49
Krymsky, A. E., 34
Kuhn, E., 36
Kusinara, 129–30

Laboulaye, E. R. Lefebvre, 12
Lalita-vistara, 12, 13
Lampros, S., 62–3
Latin, 12, 59–60
Laz, 42
Le Coq, A. von, 27
Legenda Aurea (Golden Legend), 11, 12, 47
Leo, son of John, 60

Library of Congress, Washington, 6, 44
Liebrecht, Felix, 12
Life of the Blessed Iodasaph, 44–58
Lope de Vega, 12

Magdalen College, Oxford, 62
Mahābhārata, 16
Mahāvastu, 13, 14
Mahdi, the, 129
Mahdī, caliph, 32
Makhādeva, king, 31
Mani, Manichaeans, 24–9, 32–5, 64, 130
Manṣūr, caliph, 32
Mar-Devāriāh, 33
Marcion, 29, 32
Marco Polo, 12
Marr, N. Y., 40, 44, 48
al-Masʿūdī, 28, 32, 39
Mattingly, H., 17, 47, 49, 51–6
Maximus Confessor, St., 57
Māyā, queen, 13
Mazdak, 29
Merchant of Venice, The, 5, 12
Meru, 17
Mesopotamia, 24, 29, 45, 53
Michael the Sabaite, St., 43
Milinda (Menander), king, 15–16, 26
Mirza Ghulam Ahmad, 129
Mons Admirabilis, 42
Muhammad the Prophet, 36, 41
al-Muqaffaʿ, ʿAbdullāh ibn, 31–3

Nachor, *see* Nakhor
al-Nadīm, Muhammad ibn, 27, 29, 32, 34
Nāgasena, 15, 16, 26
Nakhor, 54, 56, 58, 101, 103, 107–9
Naples, 59
Nemesius of Emesa, 57
Neo-Platonism, 37
Nepal, 26
Nerses, prince of Georgia, 41
New Testament, 36, 62
Nicholson, R. A., 36
Nihavand, Old, 33
Nine Clans, Turks of the, 27
Nino, St., 41
Nirvana, 15–17
Noble Way, the, 30
Nūr al-Dīn ibn Jīwākhān, Shaykh, 35
Nutsubidze, Shalva, 49

Oldenburg, S. von, 35, 130
Olympus, Mount, 43, 62–3

Palestine, 42–3
Pali, 13, 15
Pancatantra, 16, 31
Paris, 59
Parthian, 28
Peeters, Father Paul, 40, 44, 62
Pehlevi, 29, 31–2
Percival David Foundation of Chinese Art, 6
Persia, Persian, 24, 31–2, 34–5, 43
Petridsoni Monastery, 43
Phoenix, 32
Podro, Joshua, 129–30
Prakrit, 24
Prasenajit, king, 22
Prochorus, St., 42–5
Procopius, St., 42
Provençal, 12
Pseudo-Dionysius the Areopagite, 43
Punjab, 129
Pythagoras, 37

Qadiyan, 129
qaghan, Uigur, 27
Qaukhchishvili, S., 49
Qum, 34

Rakhis (Rakis), 39, 45, 47–8, 54, 56, 100–5
Rayy, 34
Rehatsek, E., 38
Rhys Davids, T. W., 15
Rieu, C., 35
Romaic, 12
Roman Catholic Church, 11–12
Romana Cloister, 43
Romanus, St., 42–3
Rome, 43, 129
Rosen, Baron V., 33, 44, 49
Rūmī, 31
Russian, 5

Saba, St., 11, 42, 59–60, 63
Sabaeans, 24, 28
Śākyas, 13
Samanians, 24, 30

Samarkand, 24, 29
Samuel, Monastery of St., 42
Sanskrit, 5, 13, 26, 28, 39
Saracens, 41
Sarnadib, *see* Serendib
Sasanian kings, 24
Saul, king, 56
Scandinavia, 12
School of Oriental and African Studies, London, 36, 44
Senaar, 45, 53
Serendib (Ceylon), 39, 45, 49, 52, 55–6
Shahrastānī, 30
Shakespeare, 5, 12
Shawilābaṭṭ, *see* Sūlābaṭ
Shī'a, 34
Shinar, *see* Senaar
Simeon, Monastery of St., 42
Simeon, the Monk, 33
Sinai, Mount, 42–3, 58
Sindbad, Book of, 34
Slavonic, 12
Socrates, 37
Soghdians, 24, 27–8
Sophronius of Palestine, 69
Spanish, 12
Srinagar, 129–30
Stephen, the translator, 43
Śuddhodana, king, 13, 14, 21, 27–8
Ṣūfism, 30–1
Sūlābat, 39, 45
Syria, 42–3
Syriac, 40–1, 58

al-Tahdam, 39
Tao, 62
Tê-hua porcelain, 6
Ter Nersesean, S., 44
Thedma (Theudas), 55–6, 110–12
Theodore, St., 42
Theodore, the Priest, 63
Theravāda, 13
Thessalonica, 43, 163
Theudas, *see* Thedma
Thomas, St. and Apostle, 11, 114
Tibet, Tibetan, 13, 27
Tiflis, 6, 41, 63
Toquz Oghuz Turks, 27
Tornik, John, 62
Transcaucasia, 41
Tritton, A. S., 30
Turfan, 26, 28, 35

Turkestan, 24, 27
Turks, Turkish, 27–8
Turner, Sir R. L., 44, 57

Uigurs, 27
untouchables, 28

Varazvache, John, *see* John the Athonite
Venice, 59
Vienna, 35

Wāsiṭ, 28
Weisslowits, N., 38
Weller, F., 26
Westminster, 12

Winternitz, M., 13
Woking mosque, 129
Wolff, R. L., 44, 46
Woodward, G. R., 17, 47, 49, 51–6

Younghusband, Sir F., 129
Yūdāsaf (Yus Asaf, Yūzāsaf), 29, 39, 45, 129–30
Yule, Sir Henry, 12

Zaehner, R. C., 25
Zandan (Zadan, Zardan), 53–4, 73–8, 95–6, 100–1
Zarādusht (Zoroaster), 25, 29
Zhalia Cloister, 43
zindīq, 34
zuhd, 30

For Product Safety Concerns and Information please contact our EU representative GPSR@taylorandfrancis.com
Taylor & Francis Verlag GmbH, Kaufingerstraße 24, 80331 München, Germany

www.ingramcontent.com/pod-product-compliance
Lightning Source LLC
Chambersburg PA
CBHW061844300426
44115CB00013B/2503